art / shop / eat
LOS ANGELES

Jade Chang

A note on maps. Commercial galleries, restaurants and shops are each identified with a coloured, numbered dot in the text and on the chapter maps. Some restaurants or shops that are close together may share a number to conserve space.

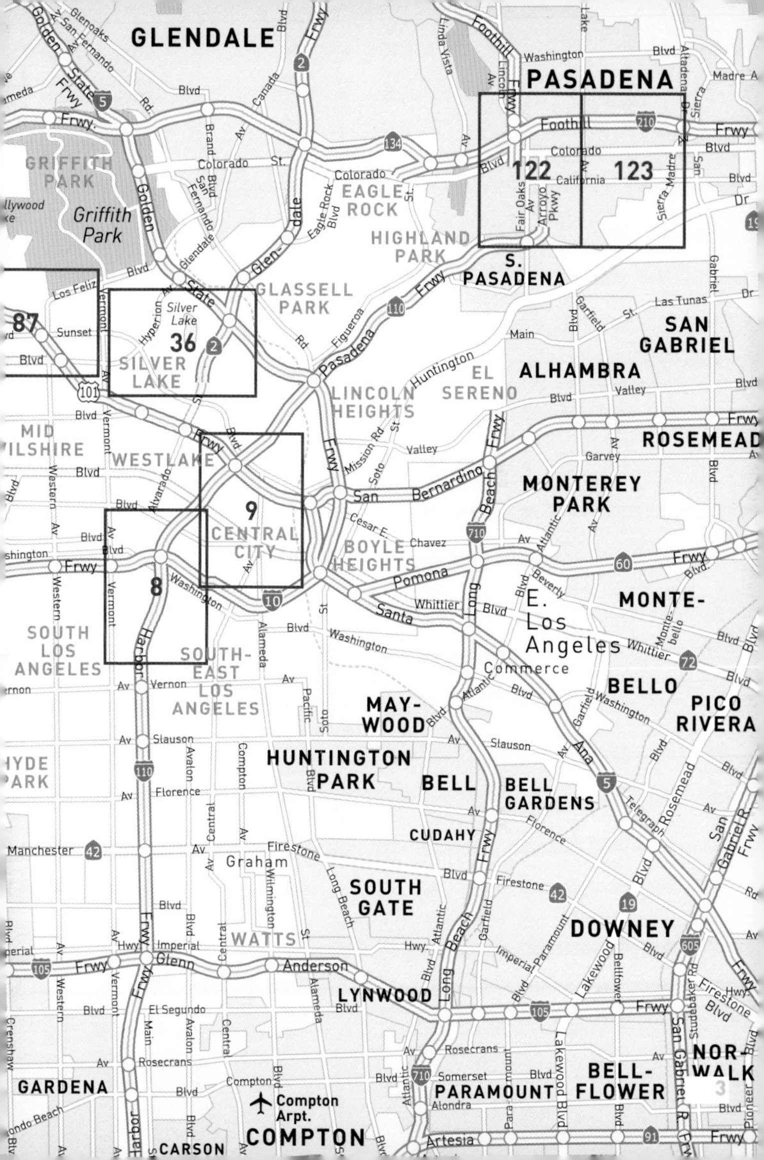

GLENDALE
PASADENA
GRIFFITH PARK
Griffith Park
EAGLE ROCK
HIGHLAND PARK
S. PASADENA
GLASSELL PARK
SAN GABRIEL
ALHAMBRA
Silver Lake
SILVER LAKE
EL SERENO
LINCOLN HEIGHTS
MID WILSHIRE
WESTLAKE
ROSEMEAD
MONTEREY PARK
CENTRAL CITY
BOYLE HEIGHTS
MONTE-
E. Los Angeles
SOUTH LOS ANGELES
SOUTH-EAST LOS ANGELES
Commerce
BELLO
PICO RIVERA
MAY-WOOD
HUNTINGTON PARK
BELL
BELL GARDENS
HYDE PARK
CUDAHY
Graham
SOUTH GATE
DOWNEY
WATTS
LYNWOOD
NOR-WALK
BELL-FLOWER
GARDENA
PARAMOUNT
Compton Arpt.
COMPTON
CARSON
122
123
87
36
9
8
3

Downtown

Santa Monica & the Westside

Hollywood & Midtown

Pasadena

CONTENTS

introduction

In Los Angeles life can be any size you choose to make it. You can be projected on a sixty-foot screen or you can shrink away in one of the hundreds of anonymous apartment blocks—it's a city of hopes and dreams, spectacular rises and spectacular falls. What could be a better subject for an artist? From the street-level murals of East LA to David Hockney's series of swimming pools, Los Angeles has long been both home and inspiration to painters and poets.

With an area of 470 square miles and a population of just under four million, Los Angeles can squeeze in every stereotype—palm trees, earthquakes, limos, gangs, malls, starlets—and still have space left for fresh ideas in urban development, a rich multicultural art scene and some of the best food on the planet.

This guidebook will take you on an art lovers' tour of Los Angeles. You'll find tips on exploring the city's five major museums—LACMA, the Getty, MOCA, the Hammer and the Norton Simon—as well as commercial galleries and architecturally significant buildings. But because thinking about life's big issues can get exhausting, we've also included plenty of fun in the area; shopping (from high-end boutiques full of custom-made clothing to discount flower markets) and eating (from the best local burger chain to the hottest Hollywood restaurant) are high on LA's list of pleasures.

You'll find that the carefully selected listings in this book are usually located near one of the art spots, either a museum or a gallery. The entertainment section gives you music, theatre, cinema and comedy club options; and with the freeway map and planning section you'll be able to negotiate LA's vast network of neighbourhoods—but to keep yourself sane, try not to do any of that negotiating during rush hour!

DOWNTOWN

NORTH UNIVERSITY PARK
EXPOSITION PARK
Natural History Museum of LA County
California African American Museum
California Science Center
Exposition Park
off map
off map
Santa Monica Frwy
Harbor Frwy
Transit
Pico
Grand
0
500 yards

CHINATOWN
Cathedral of Our Lady of the Angels
Chinese American Museum
Disney Concert Hall
Museum of Contemporary Art
Bradbury Building
Central Library
Japanese American Museum
Pershing Square
Museum of Neon Art
LITTLE TOKYO
CENTRAL CITY
Chinatown
Civic Center
Pershing Sq
7th St/Metro Center
Union Station
off map
Olvera St
Hollywood Frwy
Pasadena Frwy
Santa Ana Frwy
Santa Monica Frwy
Sunset Bl
Cesar e Chavez Av
Figueroa St
Broadway
Alameda St
Temple St
Olympic Blvd
Wilshire Blvd
0
500 yards

Downtown is the heart of Los Angeles in one sense—but then again, LA is no ordinary city, and Downtown's role in the urban landscape is far from the usual. Once it was LA, plain and simple, but as sprawl and the incorporation of outlying areas transformed the city, Downtown declined and fell into disfavour.

However, as dynamic new buildings like Frank Gehry's Disney Concert Hall (see p. 16) go up—along with the average income of Downtown's new population—the city has become increasingly interested in preserving its past. The crumbling 1920s movie palaces, built for fantasy, are being refurbished, and historic buildings are being reused rather than knocked down. Vestiges of LA's Mexican, Japanese and Chinese communities can still be found in the Olvera Street, Little Tokyo and Chinatown area that encircle Downtown's historic core, while a new generation of urban immigrants—artists, architects, web developers, entrepreneurs and the like—are claiming a place.

Downtown always had a handful of quality restaurants, thanks to the law firms and their expense accounts, but today those restaurants are getting sexier, and are being joined by bars, lounges and even the occasional designer boutique. Arts institutions like MOCA and the Philharmonic were faithful to Downtown during its empty years and they're welcoming the influx of young gallery owners, who have set up shop both in Chinatown and in the centre of Downtown. The city is at its tipping point (money is coming in, but the artists haven't been completely priced out yet) which makes it the perfect time to be a visitor and to watch as new life flowers in Downtown's historic streets.

Museum of Contemporary Art (MOCA)

OPEN	MOCA is open from 11 am–5 pm, Mon–Fri; 11 am–8 pm, Thur; 11 am–6 pm, Sat–Sun. Closed Tue and Wed.
CHARGES	Regular admission $8 (for both venues); students $5 (with ID), over 65 $5. Thursdays free
GUIDED VISITS	Three free tours daily, at 12 pm, 1 pm and 2 pm. Tours meet in the lobby of each building and last about 45 minutes. Sign-language tours are available for groups of five or more with five days notice; call (213) 621-1741.
DISABLED ACCESS	Fully wheelchair accessible, wheelchairs and strollers available at Information Desk
SERVICES	**Grand Ave** Gift shop, café, coat check. The MOCA shop opens a half-hour before the museum and closes a half-hour after. **Geffen Contemporary** Gift shop, reading room. MOCA holds regular art talks and classes. During the summer there are weekly evening parties at MOCA Grand Avenue, with DJs and drink specials. Special family events are held on the first Friday of each month. More info at the online Events Calendar or call the museum.
TELEPHONE	(213) 626-6222
WEB	www.moca.org
MAIN ENTRANCE	**Grand Ave.** 250 South Grand Avenue. **Geffen Contemporary**152 North Central Avenue.
GETTING THERE	**Grand Ave** Metrolink: Red Line to Pershing Square. By car: From the 110 freeway, take the 4th St exit, or from the 101 freeway, the Grand Ave. exit. Park in the Walt Disney Concert Hall underground lot; $8 for 3 hours with MOCA validation. Metered street parking also available. **Geffen Contemporary** Metrolink: Red Line to Civic Center. By car: From the 10 freeway, take the Alameda exit; from the 101 freeway south, the Temple exit; from the 101 north, Alameda exit. Park at the Advanced Parking Systems lot on the corner of 1st and Central, $4.25 flat rate. Metered street parking also available.

MOCA Grand Ave.

Spread across three separate buildings, two in Downtown LA and one in West Hollywood (on the grounds of the Pacific Design Center), the Museum of Contemporary Art (MOCA) presents a constantly changing series of tightly curated shows. From career retrospectives of contemporary giants like John Baldessari to architecture and design exhibitions that draw on LA's architectural gems, to the exhibition of emerging multi-media and performance artists, MOCA is intelligent, accessible and—occasionally—daring. Dedicated to work created after 1940, the museum's permanent collection includes an impressive array of photo series by Robert Frank, Diane Arbus, Lee Friedlander and Garry Winogrand.

Highlights from the permanent collection are occasionally shown, but the strength of MOCA lies in its temporary shows.

THE BUILDINGS

MOCA, born in the early 1980s, didn't plan on having separate homes. While the anchor space, now known as MOCA Grand Avenue, was under construction, the coalition of artists, donors,

civic leaders and curators that had rallied together to create the museum were eager to start the show. They leased an interim exhibition space from the city for $1 a year and hired local architect Frank Gehry to renovate it.

Gehry's renovation of the industrial site, dubbed the Temporary Contemporary, preserved skylights and exposed trusses and a wall of overhead doors, giving the museum the welcoming feel of a workshop, rather than a series of rooms. It opened in 1983 with a performance piece titled *Available Light*, with music by John Adams and sets by Gehry. Even after the main site opened, MOCA decided to keep the Temporary Contemporary, which was renovated and renamed the Geffen Contemporary after record executive David Geffen made a $5 million donation.

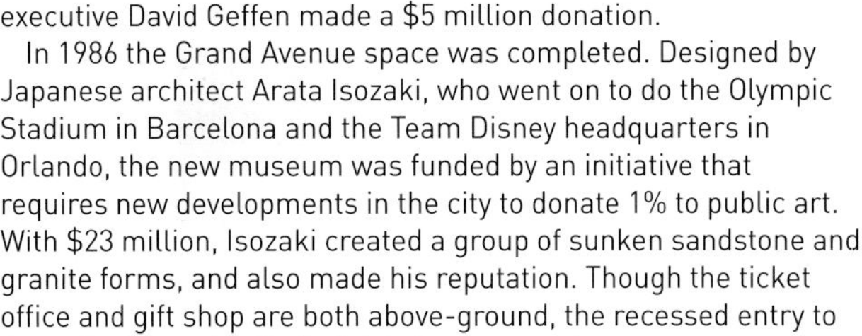

In 1986 the Grand Avenue space was completed. Designed by Japanese architect Arata Isozaki, who went on to do the Olympic Stadium in Barcelona and the Team Disney headquarters in Orlando, the new museum was funded by an initiative that requires new developments in the city to donate 1% to public art. With $23 million, Isozaki created a group of sunken sandstone and granite forms, and also made his reputation. Though the ticket office and gift shop are both above-ground, the recessed entry to the galleries and café diminish the museum's street presence.

MOCA Pacific Design Center (see p. 101) opened in 2001. Housed in a Cesar Pelli building, the satellite, which concentrates on architecture and design, gives the museum a Westside presence.

THE COLLECTION

MOCA's 5,000 pieces include work by **Jasper Johns**, **Andy Warhol**, **Robert Rauschenberg**, **Nan Goldin**, **Ed Moses** (who gave the museum 11 pieces that highlight significant points in his career), **Willem de Kooning**, **Richard Diebenkorn**, **Mark Rothko**, **Claes Oldenberg** and **Cy Twombly**. Local and California artists are especially well-represented, with work by people like **David Hockney**, **Lari Pittman**, **Catherine Opie**, **Mike Kelley**, **Robert Irwin** and **Bill Viola**.

The museum's fund for new acquisitions is relatively small, and most of the works came through bequests or as direct gifts from artists. The most significant recent addition to MOCA's permanent collection is **Ed Ruscha**'s *Chocolate Room*, the artist's only installation piece, created in 1970 for the 35th Venice Biennale. Part of the permanent collection can be viewed online; the website also features an innovative Digital Gallery.

EXHIBITION PROGRAMME

MOCA debuted its Grand Ave. building with a wide-ranging inaugural exhibition titled *Individuals: A Selected History of Contemporary Art 1945-1986*, which included over 400 works by 70 artists. In 1992 the museum put on *Helter Skelter: L.A. Art in the 1990s*, a provocative show that proved MOCA's ability to launch Southern Californian artists. Many of the stars of that powerful, dark exhibit, which featured 16 visual artists and 10 writers, are still active in the art world, including **Chris Burden**, **Mike Kelley**, **Paul McCarthy**, **Liz Larner**, **Lari Pittman**, **Nancy Rubins** and **Charles Ray**.

As part of a 1997 exhibit titled *Uncommon Sense*, the Cornerstone Theater Company, nationally known for their site-specific work involving non-actors from marginalised communities, staged a new play on a city bus inside the museum.

Recent exhibitions include a retrospective of earth artist **Robert Smithson**, whose who is best known for his influential *Spiral Jetty*, a 1,500 foot rock 'path' that extended into the Great Salt Lake. Also part of the retrospective were ephemera from Smithson's personal files, including sketches for many of his works, and previously unknown paintings, collages and drawings.

UPCOMING SHOWS

MOCA GRAND AVENUE

7/17/05–10/10/05: ***Basquiat*** is a retrospective of the graffiti art, abstract expressionism and sociopolitical themes of Brooklyn-based artist Jean-Michel Basquiat. He began his career on the

Andreas Gursky *99 Cent* (1999)

streets, became a confidant of Andy Warhol and was a larger-than-life figure in the already dramatic New York art world of the 1980s.

11/20/05–3/13/06: ***Masters: Twentieth-Century American Comics*** examines the influence of comic books and comic strips through the work of 15 masters of the form, including Will Eisner, R. Crumb, Chris Ware and Art Spiegelman.

2/05/06-4/16/06: ***Painting in Tongues*** surveys six emerging international painters who mix styles and materials, including LA artists Mark Grotjahn and Ivan Morley.

Ongoing: ***Into the Unknown: Abstraction from the Collection 1940-1960*** features important pieces from the permanent collection, including Willem de Kooning's *Two Women with Still Life* (1952) and major works by Sam Francis, Alberto Giacometti, Arshile Gorky, Franz Kline, Lee Krasner, Ad Reinhardt and Mark Rothko.

in the area

Museum of Neon Art 501 W. Olympic Blvd. [at 5th St.], (213) 489-9918, www.neonmona.org. The contemporary neon art on display mercifully goes beyond 1980s-style squiggles and lightning bolts, but it's the retro neon signage that's really worth seeing. Even better are the museum's popular double-decker bus tours, complete with cocktails and lively guides that tell the history of LA through its neon. Metro Red Line to 7th St. **Map p. 9, 1C**

Disney Concert Hall 135 N. Grand Ave. [at 1st], (213) 972-7211, www.wdch.org. Before the Guggenheim Bilbao was a glimmer in a canny museum planner's eye, architect Frank Gehry had already designed the Walt Disney Concert Hall, a symphony of titanium-hued curves that many have likened to his Spanish museum. Years of city foot-dragging held up construction, but in 2004 the concert hall, with impeccable acoustics, an enormous organ and horrendously upholstered seats (the pattern was also designed by

Frank Gehry's Walt Disney Concert Hall, home of the LA Philharmonic

Gehry), finally opened to the public. The new home of the LA Philharmonic isn't actually affiliated with the Mouse; it's named after Disney because his late wife, Rose, donated the initial $50 million. The terrace garden's rose-shaped sculpture, tiled in Delft china, is in her honour. For more info on performances, see p. 148. There are self-guided audio tours from 9 am–3 pm on non-matinee days; 9 am–10.30 am on matinee days; $10. Metro Red Line to Civic Center **Map p. 9, 2B**

Olvera Street From Alameda to E. Cedar Chavez, (213) 680-2525, www.olvera-street.com. This bustling 'old Mexico'-style marketplace forms the heart of the El Pueblo Historic Monument. Try the fresh corn tortillas at the restaurants surrounding the plaza, or get a cup of sliced mangoes with chile powder from one of the pushcart vendors. Historic buildings include the 1818 Avila Adobe, built by former mayor Francisco Avila, and the 1869 Pico House, built by the last Mexican governor of California, Pio Pico. If you're around, don't miss the Blessing of the Animals (April) or the *Dia de los Muertos* (Nov. 2) celebrations. **Map p. 9, 4B**

Japanese American National Museum 369 E. 1st St. [at Alameda], (213) 625-0414, www.janm.org. 10 am–5 pm, Tue–Sun; 10 am–8 pm, Thur. Free admission 5 pm–8 pm, Thur, and all day every third Thursday. Designed by Japanese-American architect Gyo Obata (who also did the Smithsonian's National Air and Space Museum in Washington DC), the museum covers both art and history and has an extensive archive of materials related to the WWII internment camps. Past exhibits include retrospectives of George Nakashima and Isamu Noguchi. **Map p. 9, 3B**

Chinese American Museum 425 N. Los Angeles St., (213) 626-5240, www.camla.org. 10 am–3 pm, Tue–Sun. Stop by during your Olvera Street visit for explorations of Chinese America past and present, especially in the Los Angeles area, where it has a long history. The museum located in the recently restored Garnier Building, which has been occupied by Chinese businesses since it was built in 1890. If you're in town in February, don't miss the Lantern Festival celebrations. **Map p. 9, 3-4B**

John Kwok *Kites* (1976) at the Chinese America Museum

Bradbury Building 304 S. Broadway [at 3rd St.], (213) 626-1893. This office building is a gorgeous, sunlit tower of Victorian-esque futurism. According to local lore, the building's owner, mining magnate Lewis Bradbury, hated original architect Sumner Hunt's design and handed the project over to Hunt's subordinate, George Wyman. Wyman was a complete novice, and based his design on an 1887 novel of utopian ideals called *Looking Backward*. However, Bradbury loved the building, and so did Ridley Scott, who filmed the final scenes of *Blade Runner* there. **Map p. 9, 2B**

EXPOSITION PARK - MAP P. 8, 1-2D

California Science Center 700 State Drive, 323-724-3623, www.casciencectr.org. The hands-on museum is great for kids, and also has a seven-storey IMAX theatre. In a Louvre-influenced move, the Science Center recently erected a sleek glass building behind the façade of its original 1912 structure.

Natural History Museum of Los Angeles County 900 Exposition Blvd., (213) 763-DINO, www.nhm.org. The museum juxtaposes the familiar history exhibitions—a massive T-Rex skull, a Hall of Native American Cultures, a Hall of Gems and Minerals—with inventive rotating exhibitions that often bring together artists and writers to reinterpret the museum's holdings. Admission free on the first Tuesday of each month.

California African American Museum 600 State Drive, (213) 744-7432, www.caamuseum.org. Dedicated to the history, art and culture of African-Americans, particularly in California.

The movie palaces of Broadway These lavish movie palaces, built in the 1920s and 1930s, are a paradise of gilt and chandeliers and the Greek and Egyptian motifs popular at the time. A walk down Broadway between 3rd and 9th will take you past the **Million Dollar Theatre**, the **Los Angeles Theatre**, the **Orpheum** and the **Palace**, but the best way to get inside is through the LA Conservancy's walking tours and 'Last Remaining Seats' programme, which screens classic films inside the renovated theatres. Check out their event schedule on www.laconservancy.org or call (213) 623-2489. **Map p. 9, 1-2C**

Central Library 630 W. 5th Street, (213) 228-7000, www.lapl.org/central. One of the city's best public institutions, it was completely rebuilt after the original was destroyed in a fire. Art is incorporated throughout the library building—look for the murals and 2,000-pound chandelier in the Lodwrick M. Cook Rotunda, the glass elevators lined with old cards from the card catalogue and the warm, whimsical (and enormous!) atrium chandeliers created by Therman Statom. For tour information call the docent office at (213) 228-7055 or print out the self-guided tour, available on the website. **Map p. 9, 2B**

SCIArc 960 E. 3rd Street, (213) 613-2200, www.sciarc.edu. This is one of the city's best architecture and design schools, built in the old Santa Fe Train Depot, a long, airy building that students sometimes traverse by skateboard. Gallery open 10 am–6 pm. **Map p. 9, 4C**

Watts Towers

Cathedral of Our Lady of the Angels 555 West Temple St., (213) 680-5200, www.olacathedral.org. Designed by a Pritzker Prize winner, Spanish architect Raphael Moneo, the new cathedral opened its Robert Graham-designed doors in 2002. Cardinal Robert Mahoney, the Archbishop of Los Angeles, frequently leads Mass here. If you're not interested in the sacred, there's always the well-stocked gift shop, complete with wine made by monks.
Map p. 9, 3B

Watts Towers 1727 E. 107th St., (323) 860-9964, www.watts towers.net. Folk artist Simon Rodia dedicated 33 years of his life to building skyward, constructing these 90-ft. spires on his own. They are made of twisted steel rods, embedded with a mosaic of glass, tiles, rocks and found objects. The Gaudi-like towers have become a community centre and a potent symbol of hope.
Off map

The roots of the city

The history of Los Angeles as a city began in 1781, when a group of forty-six men, women and children were persuaded by the Spanish governor of California to settle near Olvera Street's current site (see p. 17). The settlers (who were mixed, some Native American, some Spanish, some Latin American) named their new home El Pueblo de la Reina de Los Angeles, or 'The Town of Our Lady of the Angels'. By 1790, there were 28 households registered in Los Angeles, a total population of 139. This grew to 315 by 1800.

LA—indeed all of California—was ruled by Spain until 1822 and Mexico until 1848, when it became part of the US (although it became a state only in 1850).

Seonna Hong *A Little Help from my Friends* (2004) at sixspace

commercial galleries

The first artists began to move Downtown because it was one of the only places to find cheap space, and lots of it. But industrial lofts were not considered habitable by the city, and it was only when the Artists in Residence ordinance was passed in 1981 that the nucleus of old Los Angeles became a real home for artists.

In the early 1990s a new generation of artists began moving into Downtown LA's empty warehouses. With them came a vibrant gallery scene that has been both threatened and buoyed by an influx of moneyed residents and an inevitable rise in rents.

A good way to see a few galleries in one visit is to do the Downtown Art Walk, a self-guided tour that takes in galleries and exhibition spaces. See www.downtownartwalk.com for more details.

Acuna-Hansen Gallery 427 Bernard St., (323) 441-1624, www.ahgallery.com. Run by a friendly, experienced, husband-and-wife team, this gallery shows emerging and mid-career artists, including Carlee Fernandez. **Map p. 9, 4A** ❶

Bank 400 S. Main St. [at 4th St.], (213) 621-4055, www.bank-art.com. This gallery in the Old Bank District shows emerging and established contemporary artists, including Betsy Davis, Michael Schnabel, John Klima, Brody Condon and Camille Utterback. **Map p. 9, 3C** ❷

The Brewery 620 Moulton Ave [at N. Main St.], www.breweryartwalk.com. It claims to be the 'world's largest art colony', with over 500 artists living in converted lofts built in an old Pabst Blue Ribbon brewery. There are biannual open houses, and many of the studios and galleries are open to the public throughout the year. **Off map p. 9, 4A** ❸

CHUNG KING ROAD - MAP P. 9, A3 ❹

A quirky row of contemporary art galleries have moved into this Chinatown back alley. They often debut graduates of local art schools and have great street-wide summer openings. Some of the more interesting:

> Black Dragon Society 961 Chung King Rd., (213) 620-0030, www.black-dragon-society.com. Located in a former kung fu studio, often shows younger artists.
>
> China Art Objects 933 Chung King Rd., (213) 613-0384, www.chinaartobjects.com. Artist Pae White helped design this gallery, the first to open on Chung King Road. They've shown Jorge Pardo and still exhibit influential local artists.

Peres Projects 969 Chung King Rd., (213) 617-1100, www.peres-projects.com. International and American avant-garde artists.

Galeria Otra Vez 3802 Cesar E. Chavez Ave., (323) 881-6444, www.selfhelpgraphics.com. Part of Self-Help Graphics, a collaborative enterprise dedicated to promoting work by Latino and Chicano artists, the gallery also offers classes, a silk-screen shop, boutique and gallery. There's an amazing Day of the Dead celebration every Nov. 2. **Off map**

La Luz de Jesus 4633 Hollywood Blvd., (323) 666-7667, www.laluzdejesus.com. 11 am–5 pm, Mon–Wed; 11 am–9 pm, Thur–Sat; 12 pm–6 pm, Sun. Actually in Los Feliz (see p. 35), this major player in the underground arts has been in the neighbourhood since 1986, breaking artists like Manual Ocampa, Joe Coleman and Robert Williams. They have truly fun opening nights. They are also ground zero for the frequent Los Feliz art walks. **Off map p. 9, 4A** ❸

Raid Projects 602 Moulton Ave, (323) 441-9593, www.raidprojects.com. 12 am–3 pm, Sat; otherwise by appointment. This artist-run curatorial organisation hosts 12 projects a year of painting, sculpture, film, new media, digital and performance. **Map p. 36, 1B** ❻

sixspace 549 W. 23rd St.,(213) 765-0248, www.sixspace.com. 12 am–4 pm, Tue-Sat. Gallery owner Caryn Coleman is an active promoter of LA's modern art scene, and also runs the website art.blogging.la. sixspace shows Seonna Hong (see previous page), Fafi, Glenn E. Friedman, Shepard Fairey and Martin Oniveros. **Map p. 8, 3B-C** ❼

eat

RESTAURANTS

$ **Grand Central Market** 317 S. Broadway Ave. [at 3rd St.], (213) 624-2378, www.grandcentralsquare.com. Right across the street from the spectacular Bradbury Building is the place to go for a taste of history with your meal. Ever since it opened in 1917, Grand Central Market has been the major food shopping spot for

Scott Musgrove *Booted Glamour Cat* (2004) at La Luz de Jesus

Downtown residents. Even today, locals stop here for farm-fresh produce. But what the visitor wants to go for are the food stalls; wander around and you'll find zingy ceviche, amazing gorditas, briny seafood broth, old-school Chinese food and a crowded bar that serves its beers very, very cold. **Map p. 9, 2B** ❶

Señor Fish 422 E. 1st St. [at Alameda], (213) 625-0566. A brightly coloured storefront across the street from the Japanese American National Museum, this tasty taqueria serves up boatloads of its speciality: crispy battered fish folded into fresh tortillas then topped with cabbage and a generous streak of white sauce. Fish tacos are a speciality of Baja, but they make some LA concessions with vegetarian choices. On sunny afternoons, the back patio is full of office workers and Little Tokyo natives bearing loaded plates of lobster burritos. **Map p. 9, 3-4C** ❷

Groundworks Coffee 811 Traction Ave. [at Alameda], (213) 626-8650. Groundworks has brought street life to this stretch of Traction Ave., and is more a neighbourhood anchor than a simple place to get a cup of coffee. There's fresh-squeezed orange juice, plus an array of sandwiches—stuffed with things like pesto and fresh mozzarella—to fuel the hardworking students of SciARC (see p. 19). **Map p. 9, 4C** ❸

Mama's Hot Tamales 2124 W. 7th St., (213) 487-7474, www.mamas-hot-tamales.com. In a bid to reclaim MacArthur Park from shady drug dealers, an ambitious community group is sending out pushcart vendors, some of whom sell tamales from Mama's, an inviting café and neighbourhood centre right next to the park. Besides including a bookstore stocked with Latino literature, Mama's is also a training ground for aspiring cooks and restaurant owners. They may be still in training, but they turn out an excellent menu of tamales from across Latin America, as well as perfectly flavoured *mole* and a comforting café breakfast. Open only for breakfast and lunch. **Off map p. 9, 1B** ❹

Phillipe's 1001 N. Alameda St., (213) 628-3781, www.phillipes.com. 6 am–10 pm. You can't eat your way through Downtown LA without running into the Great French Dip debate. Phillipe's says they invented it; Cole's, a bar and restaurant in a slightly grittier part of town, also claims the soggy honours. Whoever first dipped a French roll piled high with sliced meat into a pan of *jus*, it's still the truth that Phillipe's sawdust floors, post-Dodger game crowds, surprisingly good wines and trademark horseradish mustard give it the clear edge. Step up to the counter, order a beef dip with a side of potato salad and slide into one of the long communal tables—Angelenos have been eating side-by-side here since 1908. **Map p. 9, 4A** ⑤

$$ **Angelique** 840 S. Spring St. [at 8th St.], (213) 623-8698. Unexpectedly, a French café in the heart of the Garment District. Angelique rivals fancier and more fêted Westside restaurants for the sheer perfection of its food. Portions are large: the charcuterie platter comes loaded with a selection of saucisson and three different pâtés, all of which are perfect with the cheese platter and a bottle of crisp white wine (except Angelique has no liquor licence, so you have to bring your own). Coffee and flaky croissants are also delicious. Only open for breakfast and lunch, so make sure to arrive before 3:30! **Map p. 9, 2C** ⑥

Empress Pavilion 988 Hill St., (213) 617-9898. Located on the second floor of a Chinatown plaza, the dim sum spot is the perfect alternative to yet another French toast and mimosa brunch. Uniformed servers push steaming metal carts filled with little servings of scallop dumplings, pork shu mai, shrimp stuffed peppers, radish cakes and more—they'll open the baskets and let you examine the contents so that you don't accidentally end up with a plate of chicken feet if you don't want them. The enormous dining room usually fills up quickly on weekends, so get your dim sum fix on a weekday or get there early. **Map p. 9, 4A** ⑦

Langer's Deli 704 S. Alvarado St. [at 7th], (213) 483-8050. For all the New Yorkers pining after Katz's or 2nd Avenue Deli, pull up to this pastrami paradise perched incongruously on the edge of MacArthur Park. Fresh rye bread, crusty on the outside and soft on the inside, piled high with dense, peppered meat that has a tasty streak of fat (like all real pastrami) and crunchy coleslaw—the perfect deli sandwich. The service may be from the 'waiter is always right' era and the prices are not low, but the honest food keeps customers coming back. **Off map p. 9, 1B** ⑧

$$$ **Café Pinot** 700 W. 5th St. [at Flower], (213) 239-6500. One of the best places to be on a breezy summer night is under the stars and skyscrapers that canopy Café Pinot's twinkling outdoor courtyard. On the grounds of the Central Library, this is a popular after-work spot for high-powered suits or pre-show stop for Disney Hall concertgoers (there's even a shuttle that runs between the two). **Map p. 9, 2B** ⑨

ChoSun Galbee 3330 W. Olympic Blvd., (323) 734-3330, www.chosungalbee.com. This upscale Korean BBQ restaurant is slightly outside of the Downtown area, but any carnivore who fails to take advantage of Koreatown's many excellent BBQ spots has not fully experienced LA. Order *Galbee Jumulluk* (marinated boneless short ribs) or *Bulgogi* (tender, thinly sliced marinated beef) and you'll receive a platter of beef ready to be cooked on the tabletop grills. The waitresses often take over for non-Korean patrons, but you can opt to handle the grilling yourself. The meat is accompanied by *banchan*, an assortment of little platters of kimchee, sprouted soy beans in sesame oil, spicy radishes and the like, as well as rice and soup. There aren't many vegetarian options, but fish eaters will still find plenty on the menu. **Off map p. 8, 3A** 10

Ciudad 445 S. Figueroa St. [at 4th St.], (213) 486-5171, www.ciudad-la.com. This Nuevo-Latino spot has the best happy hour (weekdays 3 pm–7 pm) in town. Carefully made mojitos and sweet-and-sour Piscoritas are just $4, along with more-than-snack-sized servings of Cubano sandwiches and fish tacos. On the regular menu are plump little bundles of green corn tamales and a changing array of dishes inspired by celebrity chefs Mary Sue Milliken and Susan Feniger's travels in Latin America. The restaurant occasionally holds cooking classes (check their website for more info). **Map p. 9, 1B** 11

Noe 251 S. Olive St. [at 2nd], (213) 356-4100. The drawing card at Noe, respected chef Robert Gadsby's new American/French/ Japanese spot in Little Tokyo's Omni Hotel, is his adventurous presentation. Courses are often accompanied by miniature drinks meant to enhance the flavours of the food; the Mimosa Salad, for example, comes paired with a Minted Mango Frappe. Gadsby's cuisine is well-suited to the tasting menu and Noe offers two, a six-course ($65) and a nine-course ($95). It's located near MOCA (see p. 11) and Disney Hall (see p. 16). **Map p. 9, 2B** 12

R-23 923 E. Second St. #109, (213) 687-7178. You'll feel like an urban adventurer when you search out R-23, a stylish sushi bar located in the heart of the Warehouse District. Skilful chefs lay out fresh slabs of tuna, salmon and albacore, as well as more exotic varieties like Hokki clam and Japanese favourite *toro*. There are plenty of choices for any no-raw-fish contingent, too, including a very rare beef tataki and big scallops grilled in their shells. **Map p. 9, 4C** 13

Traxx 800 N. Alameda St. [at Cesar Chavez], (213) 625-1999. Traxx is the best excuse to go to Union Station, Downtown's main train terminal, a 1939 mix of Mission and Art Deco that is one of LA's most beautiful buildings. Dine on the lovely outdoor patio or, even better, right in the station, on chef Tara Thomas' 'New American' cuisine (like prosciutto-stuffed pork chops and gorgonzola-crusted beef tenderloin). **Map p. 9, 4B** 14

Water Grill 544 South Grand Ave. [at 5th Ave.], (213) 891-0900. Born in an era of power lunches and three-piece suits, the Water Grill is still the top seafood restaurant in all of Los Angeles. Exquisite ingredients help—they are so integral that the dishes are simply listed by type and origin of seafood, including Alaskan Day-Boast Halibut and New Zealand John Dory. Service is also exquisite. If you're in a hurry, stop by the oyster bar for a half-dozen Hama Hamas on the half shell and a glass of bubbly. **Map p. 9, 2B** 15

BARS

Golden Gopher 417 W. Eighth St. [at Hill St.], (213) 614-8001. A piece of noir LA reimagined for the 21st C, this dark narrow bar hung with sparkling chandeliers leads out to a tiny gem of a patio with enormous sofas and strictly skyward views. A perfect mix of gritty and glam. **Map p. 9, 1C** 16

Rooftop of the Standard 550 S. Flower St. [at 6th St.], (213) 892-8080. People really do dive into the pool at this bar on top of the Standard Hotel (see p. 175), sometimes as a result of too many Red-Bull-and-vodkas and a particularly stimulating session in the multiple-person waterbed pods. The bar has amazing skyline views, stiff drinks (for a stiff price) and a hard-partying clientele. **Map p. 9, 2B** 17

Hotel Figueroa 939 S. Figueroa St. [at 9th St.], (213) 627-8971. This Moroccan wonderland blocks away from the Staples Center, a sports and concert arena, is often booked for studio wrap parties and the like. There's a quiet bar on the second floor, perfect for scotch and deep conversation, and a more social scene out by the pool. (See p. 29 for more on Hotel Figueroa). **Map p. 8, 4A** 18

Hop Louie 950 Mei Ling Way [at Hill St.], (213) 628-4244. Do your drinking in a pagoda! A local Chinatown watering hole since

Hollywood's glamour days, where the drinks are still cheap and the company good. It's a mix of old folks telling stories and young hipsters ready to challenge you to a game of gin rummy. **Map p. 9, 4A** 19

Mountain Bar 475 Gin Ling Way [at Hill St.], (213) 625-7500. Art kids drink in the red-tile glow of local architect/artist Jorge Pardo's merry modernism. Across the way is an elaborate wishing well, and a few steps away are the Chung King Road galleries (see p. 23). The Mountain Bar is often the site of readings and LA Forum for Art and Architecture events (check out www.laforum.org). **Map p. 9, 4A** 20

shop

ACCESSORIES & GIFTS

Farmacia Million Dollar 301 S. Broadway Ave. [at 3rd St.], (213) 687-3688. In the Million Dollar Theatre building, right next door to Grand Central Market, this fantastic *botanica* has the cure for whatever ails you. A pharmacist dispenses prescription medicine, but if you're looking for love or fortune, it might be best to turn to the rows of incense, candles, herbs and potions. A product of melting-pot America, these health and spiritual centres combine elements of Santeria, Catholicism and folk medicine. **Map p. 9, 2B** 1

Wing Hop Fung 727 N. Broadway Ave., (213) 626-7200, www.winghop fung.com. Packages of ginseng, top-of-the-line rice steamers, super-strength Tiger Balm, silk cheongsam dresses, little packages of Botan rice candy, hot roasted chestnuts—find it all at this enormous emporium, where the cheap and cheerful wrestles for space with the staggeringly ornate. An extensive selection of Chinese herbal remedies, with a few English-speaking herbalists. **Map p. 9, 3-4A** 2

Fugetsu-do 315 E. First St., (213) 625-8595, www.fugetsu-do.com. A hundred-year-old shop selling exquisitely made *mochi* (a sticky rice

shop

sweet, often stuffed with bean paste) desserts. An assorted box makes an excellent gift, or you can just eat them yourself as you wander through Little Tokyo. There is a nice history of the shop on the website. **Map p. 9, 3B** 3

ALSO

The Flower District 766 Wall St. [at 7th St.], (213) 627-3696, www.laflowerdistrict.com. 8 am–12 pm, Mon, Wed, Fri; 6 am–12 pm, Tue, Thur, Sat. Opens to the trade in the wee hours, then lets the public in (for $2 on weekdays, $1 on Sat) to snatch up very discounted flowers. One visit to the market, started in 1913 by Japanese growers, and you'll never pay $50 for a dozen roses again; get them here for a quarter the price, along with an wide variety of cut-rate orchids, and everything from potted ferns to flower-arranging accessories. **Map p. 9, 2C** 4

The Jewellery District Between 5th St., 8th St., Broadway Ave. and Olive St. There is no end to the bling on display here. The outside layer of stores are given over to rows and rows of gold jewellery, but as you venture further towards Hill between 6th and 7th there are dazzling displays of precious stones and elaborate pieces in the more upscale stores. A little bargaining is expected, though some of the shops peg the price to the current cost of gold. **Map p. 9, 2C** 5

CLOTHES

American Apparel 374 E. Second Street, (213) 687-0467, www.americanapparel.net (other Los Angeles locations listed on the website). Here's where it all began. Once a hip little T-shirt maker, now a clothing industry heavyweight, American Apparel is an anti-sweatshop manufacturer that quickly found favour with progressive designers, who also like its commitment to recycling scraps and phasing in organic cottons. They've recently gone global, but this Little Tokyo shop just blocks away from the original factory sells brightly coloured basics in cool cuts. **Map p. 9, 3C** 6

FIDM Scholarship Store 919 S. Grand Ave., (213).624-1200. Discounted bolts of fabric, loads of off-season Custo Barcelona and the occasional student creation crowd this bare-bones store, attached to the new Fashion Institute of Design and Merchandising campus not far from the Staples Center. A portion of proceeds go to scholarships for FIDM students. Manufacturers donate their overruns and retailers send in their unsold merchandise, which means shockingly low prices, if you're willing to do a lot of digging for the good stuff. **Map p. 9, 1C** 7

shop

The once-glorious Roxie Theater on Broadway

California Mart 110 East 9th Street, (213) 630-3600, www.californiamart.com. LA is the largest garment production centre in the country, and a lot of those clothes make their way to retailers through the 1,000-plus showrooms in the California Market Center. Usually open only to the trade, showrooms traditionally have public sample sales on the last Friday of every month (unless it conflicts with one of the many Market events) and every Friday in December. **Map p. 9, 2C** 8

Santee Alley East of Santee St., between Olympic Blvd. and 11th St. 10 am–6 pm. Despite half-hearted warnings from policemen and occasional lawsuit threats, the brazen knock-off merchants of Santee Alley virtually bowl you over with their heavily monogrammed Vuitton bags. Besides Vuitton and Prada, Kate Spade and Gucci seem to be the most popular, but we did catch a glimpse of something vaguely Marc Jacobs-like. Could-be-brand sunglasses also abound, and are often even more successful at looking real. **Map p. 9, 1D** 9

ON THE WAY: SILVER LAKE, LOS FELIZ & ECHO PARK

Once barely a blip on the sprawl-radar, Silver Lake has quickly transformed into one of the most distinctive and desirable areas in Los Angeles, with rolling hills, cosy Craftsman-style homes and a shimmering reservoir. Tucked roughly between Downtown and Hollywood, Silver Lake and neighbouring enclaves Los Feliz and Echo Park span the cultural palette: there are Armenian and Latino populations, a boho artist contingent, film industry heavyweights, pensioners and other assorted characters (now there's even a TV series, created by Aaron Spelling). It may lack the polish of Beverly Hills, but Silver Lake more than compensates with its mix of laidback eateries, store-front galleries, and boutiques helmed by local designers on the make.

One of the main shopping districts is Vermont Ave. (Map p. 36, 1A-B) near Hollywood Blvd. For shoe maniacs, few stores rival **Camille Hudson** (4685 Hollywood Blvd.), who makes spiky heels in electric colours and stocks a sneaker collection from Europe. For homeware, check out the chic and addictively minimalist **Show** (1722 North Vermont Ave.); **Wacko** (4633 Hollywood Blvd.) is a joyful mix of art books and kitsch (think lawn flamingos) with a gallery in the back. **Una Mae's** (4651 Kingswell Ave.) entices with a mix of vintage and newer-but-trendy lines like Syrup.

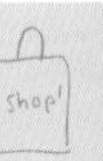

Hats at Pull My Daisy

Further west is one of the best restaurants in the area, the sparsely decorated **Kitchen** (4348 W. Sunset Blvd.), with delicious pistachio-crusted salmon. At the heart of Silver Lake is Sunset Junction, the area where Santa Monica Blvd. empties into Sunset Blvd. **Café Stella** (3932 Sunset Blvd.) is a warm-weather must with

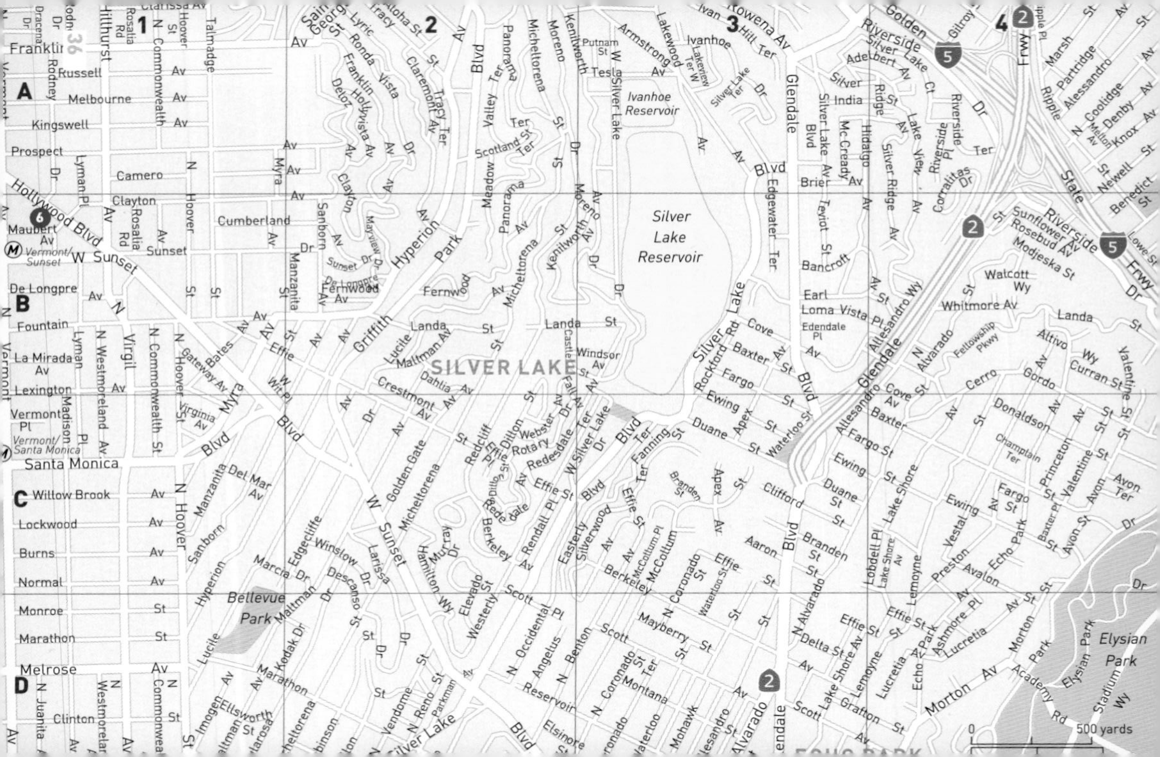

Silver Lake Reservoir
Ivanhoe Reservoir
SILVER LAKE
Elysian Park
Bellevue Park
Glendale Blvd
W Sunset Blvd
Hyperion Av
Griffith Park Blvd
Silver Lake Blvd
W Silver Lake Dr
Rowena Av
Riverside Dr
Golden State Frwy
Glendale Frwy
Santa Monica Blvd
Hollywood Blvd
N Hoover St
N Commonwealth Av
N Virgil Av
N Westmoreland Av
Vermont Av
Fountain Av
Melrose Av
Lyman Pl
Madison Av
Hillhurst Av
Franklin Av
Myra Av
Manzanita St
Sanborn Av
Clayton Av
Effie St
Micheltorena St
Lucile Av
Landa St
Berkeley Av
Scott Av
Alvarado St
Echo Park Av
Lake Shore Av
Morton Av
Academy Rd
Stadium Wy
Vermont/Sunset
Vermont/Santa Monica
500 yards
A
B
C
D
1
2
3
4
36

its romantic courtyard seating and upscale French cuisine. For locally made jewellery like Dean watches, clever buttons and sassy one-off T-shirts, **Pull My Daisy** (3908 Sunset Blvd.) will do the trick; **Matrushka** (3528 Sunset Blvd.) is a bastion of cutting-edge fashion that will customise anything. For soul, jazz or reggae, rifle through the bins at **Upon Shop** (3910 Sunset Blvd.). At **Casbah Café** (3900 Sunset Blvd.), you can munch on baklava before browsing through the beautiful selection of North African dresses and fabrics. **Millie's** (3524 Sunset Blvd.) is a hot breakfast spot with imaginative scrambles and pillowy biscuits, devoured by the neighbourhood's young and fashionable.

Silver Lake Boulevard boasts **Netty's** (1700 Silver Lake Blvd.), a Cajun-influenced eatery in a lush greenhouse-like setting, and **Spaceland** (1717 Silver Lake Blvd.), a rock venue known for nurturing the career of Beck.

Head east on Sunset and Silver Lake gives way to Echo Park, once a location for countless movies, now the colourful gateway to LA's largely Latino East Side. Dodger Stadium draws ardent crowds while palatial Elysian Park soothes the masses. Antique stores like **Rumer B** (2209 Sunset Blvd.) and **Minnette's** (2205 Sunset Blvd.) are perfect for Sunday-afternoon digging; boutiques like **The Kids Are Alright** (2201 W. Sunset Blvd.) and **Sirens & Sailors** (1102 Mohawk St.) dress the neighbourhood's rock-and-roll twentysomethings. **33 1/3 Books and Gallery** (1200 North Alvarado St.) has irreverent books and racks of counter-culture magazines; the **Echo Park Film Center** (1200 North Alvarado St., #C) hosts screenings.

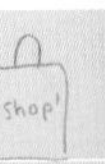

Largely residential Echo Park Ave. offers a cluster of independent shops and galleries known for throwing occasional soirees: **White Lions** (1533 Echo Park Ave.) is an Asian couture shop and **Ojala** (1547 Echo Park Ave.), a gallery that seems like a friend's well-decorated apartment, is a neighbourhood anchor.

PUBLIC ART IN THE CITY OF ANGELS

Inspired by the Mexican traditions of the city, murals abound in LA, especially Downtown and to the east. The most famous and most controversial mural is **David Alfaro Siqueiros'** *America Tropical* (1932) on Olvera Street (Map p. 9, 4B). It was commissioned by the Plaza Art Center, which was expecting an exotic Latin American jungle. Instead, the dedicated Marxist Siqueiros depicted a crucified Indian under an eagle of imperialism, with ruined pyramids in the background. The mural was so sensational that it was immediately whitewashed and then blocked by a new wall and virtually forgotten. However, as the whitewash peeled off in the 1960s, the mural was rediscovered. The mural recently underwent an extensive renovation funded by the Getty Foundation.

Another Olvera Street mural is the *Blessing of the Animals* (1978; see picture opposite) by California-born illustrator and painter **Leo Politi**. The mural shows San Antonio de Abad (St Anthony Abbot) blessing the animals, a ceremony that has been recreated at Olvera Street since 1930 (the animals are currently blessed by LA's Cardinal Mahoney). Look for Politi's own dogs in the mural, under the stairs.

Also Downtown is the Victor Clothing Building off Broadway (240 N. Broadway; Map p. 9, 3B), which is being converted into lofts but maintains its famous murals, including the giant dancing Anthony Quinn. Farmer John's, a nearby meat-processing plant in Vernon, is decorated with pastoral scenes of 'Hog Heaven' in one of the country's largest murals (3049 E. Vernon Ave.; off map).

Strangely, the freeways are always a good place to spot art—the murals along the 101 Hollywood Freeway as it passes through Downtown depict jumping kids, fuzzy cars, and, most inexplicably, fragments of a Greek temple hurtling towards

Leo Politi *The Blessing of the Animals* (1974–78)

space. Many were restored in 2003, wear and tear having taken their toll. There is also a substantial amount of beautiful graffiti.

In Santa Monica, at the Ocean Park Blvd. underpass at 4th St. (Map p. 42, 3D), a mural shows horses escaping from Santa Monica's historic pier carousel (see p. 69). Opposite, photo-realistic whales glide through a populated sea. Last year, the city government approved funds to preserve both murals.

Nearly all the commercial plazas Downtown, from the office towers at Bunker Hill to the government buildings and the Music Center, have some public art, mostly as a result of the city's '1% for Art' programme, which requires a portion of construction costs to be dedicated to public art. Most notably, a Calder arches away at the top of Bunker Hill (Map p. 9, 3A) while some Noguchi stones stand stoically around the Japanese-American Cultural Center in Little Tokyo (Map p. 9, 3B).

Also in Little Tokyo, on First St. (Map p. 9, 3B), stands a replica of the camera of Toyo Miyatake, a Japanese-American photographer who was interned during WWII. The LA Times parking structure on Spring St. (Map p. 9, 2C) features a relief showing the evolution of printing. Adjacent to the Bradbury Building, the miniscule Biddy Mason Park chronicles the life of a black midwife and leading citizen of LA in murals and reliefs.

And look out for the space invaders! French artist Space Invader has launched an international invasion, and LA is lucky to have quite a few cute little tile aliens in our midst. To get you started, there's one on Chung King Road (see p. 23), but the rest you'll have to find for yourself.

Public art is less concentrated outside Downtown, but progressive cities like Santa Monica and West Hollywood (especially around the Pacific Design Center, see p. 101) have quite a few pieces. The subway system itself can function as a gallery; the MetroArt program is constantly seeking California-based artists for new projects. LA's Cultural Affairs Department, which runs Barnsdall Art Park and numerous other art spaces, somehow manages to fund a wide array of top-notch public art while constantly being in danger of having their budget slashed. They are currently starting a programme to incorporate art at new fire stations and bridges.

For more about public art in LA, *Urban Surprises*, published by the local Balcony Press, is a good guide.

WEST LA & SANTA MONICA

SANTA MONICA
Santa Monica Museum of Art
Camera Obscura
Singing Beach Chairs
Santa Monica Pier
Pacific Ocean
Wilshire Blvd
Santa Monica Blvd
Broadway
Colorado Av
Olympic Blvd
Cloverfield Blvd
Lincoln Blvd
Pico Blvd
Ocean Av
Main St
Palisades Beach Rd
Ocean Front Wk
Montana Av
California Av
Arizona Av
Santa Monica Frwy
off map
500 yards
500 metres

Santa Monica Airport
SANTA MONICA
MAR VISTA
VENICE
OCEAN PARK
Venice Canals
off map
Lincoln Blvd
Venice Blvd
Ocean Park Blvd
Walgrove Av
Rose Av
Palms Blvd
Beethoven St
Main St
Neilson Wy
Barnard Wy
Ocean Front Wk
Pacific Av
California Av
Abbot Kinney Blvd
Washington Wy
Santa Clara Av
Donald Douglas Lp N
Donald Douglas Lp S
emar Center the Arts
500 yards
500 metres
1
2
3
4
A
B
C
D

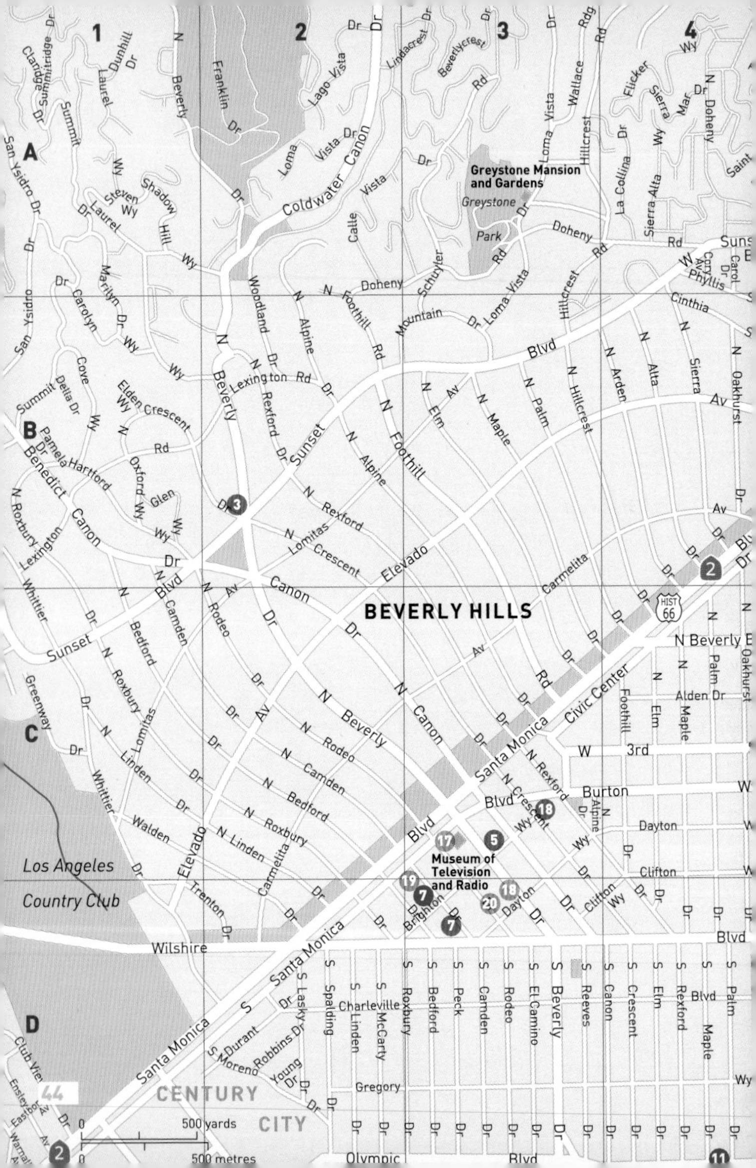
BEVERLY HILLS
Greystone Mansion and Gardens
Greystone Park
Museum of Television and Radio
Los Angeles Country Club
CENTURY CITY
Sunset Blvd
Santa Monica Blvd
Wilshire Blvd
Olympic Blvd
Coldwater Canyon Dr
Benedict Canyon Dr
Civic Center Dr
Doheny Rd
Mountain Dr
Lexington Rd
Elevado Av
Carmelita Av
Burton Wy
Dayton Wy
Clifton Wy
Brighton Wy
Charleville Blvd
Gregory Wy
N Beverly Dr
N Canon Dr
N Rodeo Dr
N Camden Dr
N Bedford Dr
N Roxbury Dr
N Linden Dr
N Crescent Dr
N Rexford Dr
N Alpine Dr
N Foothill Rd
N Elm Dr
N Maple Dr
N Palm Dr
N Hillcrest Rd
N Arden Dr
N Alta Dr
N Sierra Dr
N Oakhurst Dr
S Beverly Dr
S Santa Monica Blvd
0 500 yards
0 500 metres
1 2 3 4
A B C D

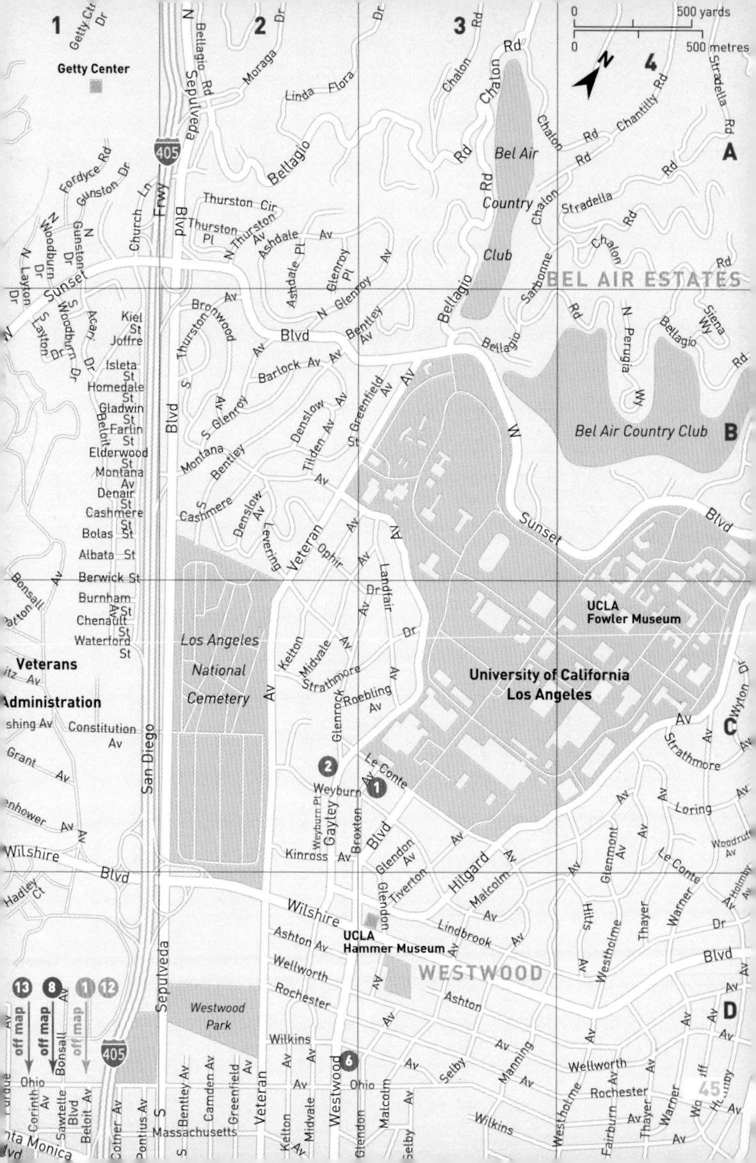
1
2
3
4
A
B
C
D
0 500 yards
0 500 metres
Getty Center
Bel Air Country Club
BEL AIR ESTATES
Los Angeles National Cemetery
Veterans Administration
University of California Los Angeles
UCLA Fowler Museum
UCLA Hammer Museum
WESTWOOD
Westwood Park
405
Sepulveda Blvd
San Diego Frwy
Sunset Blvd
Wilshire Blvd
Veteran Av
Westwood Blvd
Gayley Av
Hilgard Av
Le Conte Av
Strathmore Dr
Bellagio Rd
Chalon Rd
Stradella Rd
Chantilly Rd
Moraga Dr
Linda Flora
Thurston Cir
Ashdale Av
Glenroy Av
Bentley Av
Barlock Av
Greenfield Av
Tilden Av
Denslow Av
Montana Av
Cashmere St
Levering Av
Ophir Dr
Landfair Av
Kelton Av
Midvale Av
Roebling Av
Glenrock Av
Weyburn Av
Broxton Av
Kinross Av
Glendon Av
Tiverton Av
Malcolm Av
Lindbrook Dr
Ashton Av
Wellworth Av
Rochester Av
Wilkins Av
Ohio Av
Massachusetts Av
Selby Av
Manning Av
Westholme Av
Hilts Av
Glenmont Av
Thayer Av
Warner Av
Loring Av
Fairburn Av
Constitution Av
Grant Av
Bonsall Av
Sawtelle Blvd
Beloit Av
Cotner Av
Pontius Av
Corinth Av
Santa Monica Blvd
off map
45

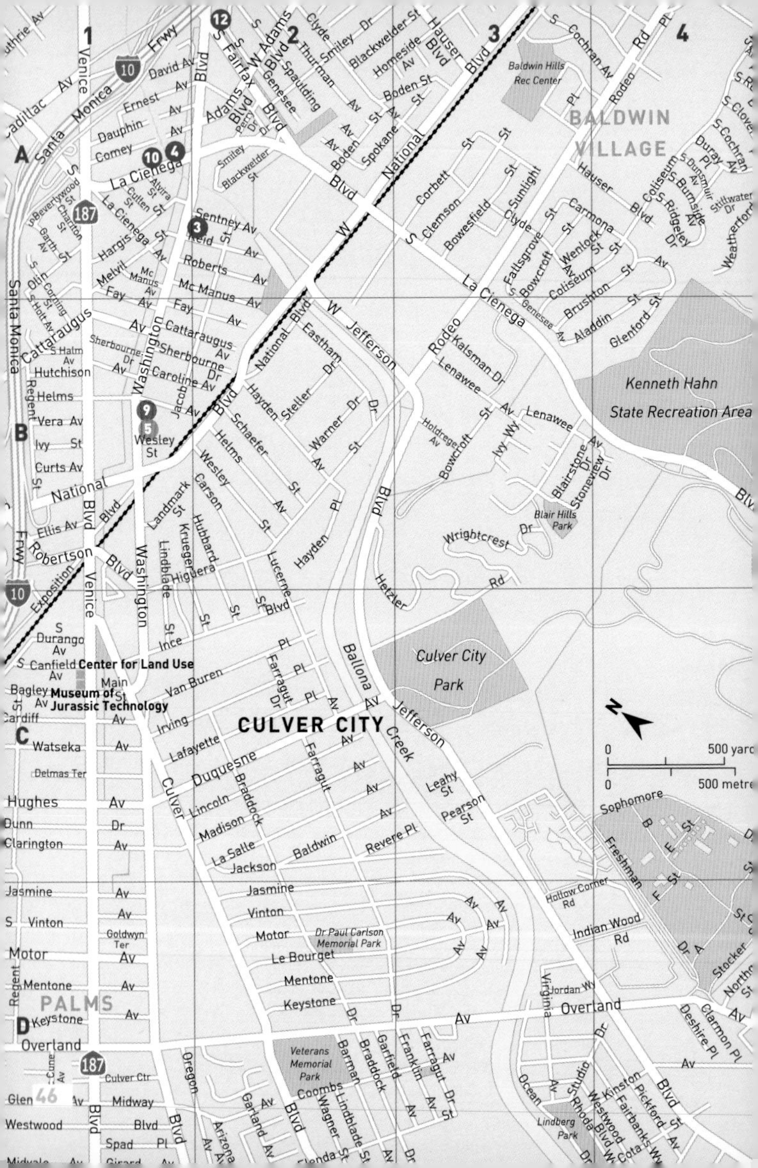
1
2
3
4
A
B
C
D
10
187
BALDWIN VILLAGE
Baldwin Hills Rec Center
Kenneth Hahn State Recreation Area
Blair Hills Park
Culver City Park
CULVER CITY
Center for Land Use
Museum of Jurassic Technology
Dr Paul Carlson Memorial Park
Veterans Memorial Park
Lindberg Park
PALMS
0
500 yards
500 metres
Santa Monica Frwy
Venice Blvd
La Cienega Blvd
Washington Blvd
National Blvd
W Jefferson Blvd
Robertson Blvd
Exposition Blvd
S Fairfax Av
W Adams Blvd
Rodeo Rd
Hauser Blvd
S Cochran Av
Coliseum St
Overland Av
Culver Blvd
Ballona Creek
Jefferson Blvd
Higuera St
Hayden Pl
Landmark St
Wesley St
Hetzler Rd
Wrightcrest Dr
Lenawee Av
Kalsman Dr
Bowcroft St
Ivy Wy
Blairstone Dr
Stoneview Dr
Cattaraugus Av
Sherbourne Dr
Caroline Av
Hutchison Av
Helms Av
Vera Av
Ivy St
Curts Av
Ellis Av
Ince Blvd
Van Buren Pl
Irving Pl
Lafayette Pl
Duquesne Av
Farragut Dr
Lincoln Av
Madison Av
La Salle Av
Braddock Dr
Jackson Av
Baldwin Av
Revere Pl
Jasmine Av
Vinton Av
Motor Av
Le Bourget Av
Mentone Av
Keystone Av
Hughes Av
Dunn Dr
Clarington Av
Watseka Av
Delmas Ter
Cardiff Av
Bagley Av
Canfield Av
Durango Av
Goldwyn Ter
Culver Ctr
Midway
Westwood Blvd
Glen Av
Spad Pl
Oregon
Arizona Av
Gartland Av
Coombs Av
Wagner
Lindblade St
Barman Av
Garfield Av
Franklin Av
Virginia Av
Jordan Wy
Studio Dr
Ocean Av
Rhoda
Kinston
Fairbanks Wy
Pickford St
Cota
Deshire Pl
Clarmon Pl
Sophomore
Freshman
Hollow Corner Rd
Indian Wood Rd
Leahy St
Pearson St
Stocker
Sentney Av
Reid St
Roberts Av
Mc Manus Av
Fay Av
Melvil Av
Hargis St
Alvira St
Cutler St
Corbett St
Clemson St
Bowesfield St
Sunlight Pl
Clyde Av
Fallsgrove St
Wenlock St
Carmona Av
Brushton St
Aladdin St
Glenford St
Genesee Av
Eastham Dr
Steller Dr
Warner Dr
Schaefer St
Carson St
Hubbard St
Krueger St
Lindblade St
Lucerne Av
Holdrege Av
Boden St
Spokane St
Smiley Dr
Blackwelder St
Homeside Av
Thurman Av
Spaulding Av
David Av
Ernest Av
Dauphin Av
Comey Av
Cadillac Av
Guthrie Av

In West LA and the cities it surrounds—Santa Monica, Beverly Hills and Culver City—skyscrapers are traded for lush lawns, noir atmosphere for the white sands of the beach. It's populated by the bejewelled dowagers of Beverly Hills and their next-door neighbours, the hard-working UCLA students of Westwood, by the happy yuppie families of Santa Monica and the boho beach bums of Venice.

West Los Angeles's two centres of art are the UCLA Hammer museum—on the edge of Westwood Village, a place that should be much more dynamic given the number of college students in the area—and the spare, hilltop Getty Center. But most of the creation doesn't happen near the Hammer or in the rarified air of the Getty; on the Westside new art is made in the warehouses of Venice and the garages-turned-studios of Culver City.

Santa Monica, which is technically its own city, is an excellent example of liberal policies played out in a real place; since cleaning up its bay, the city has been ahead of the curve in sustainability and liveability. Venice is a more recently gentrified beach town, still holding on to its image as a gritty, run-down neighbourhood with an exciting scene, while Culver City is full of young, hopeful couples just having bought their first houses. Yes, Beverly Hills is flash—full of Bentleys and trophy wives—but there is also a cosy, old side to Beverly Hills, and residents that might opt for a deli sandwich over a diamond ring.

It's a big area to cover, but the freeways are good and it's easy to find your way around, so don't hesitate.

Getty Center

OPEN The Getty Center is open from 10 am–6 pm, Tue–Thur and Sun; 10 am–9 pm, Fri and Sat. Closed Mon.

CHARGES Admission is free.

GUIDED VISITS Free daily tours: Architecture, Collection Highlights, Current Exhibition, Getty Garden, Object-in-Focus (a 15-minute look at a work of art) and general orientation. Event guides available as you exit the tram, or check website. Weekly gallery talks by the curator and conservator, Weds at 1 pm, require advance sign-up at the Information Desk.

DISABLED ACCESS Fully wheelchair accessible. Wheelchairs and strollers available at the Lower Tram Station and at the coat check. Free sign language interpretation available on request, at least ten days in advance. Audioguide for blind visitors

SERVICES Bookstore and two specialised gift shops; restaurant and café. Research Library, Teacher Resource Center and Conservation Institute. Tram from parking garage to museum. An electric vehicle charging station is available.

TELEPHONE (310) 440-7300, for hearing-impaired (310) 440-7305

WEB www.getty.edu

MAIN ENTRANCE 1200 Getty Center Drive

GETTING THERE By bus: No. 761.
By car: From the 405 freeway take the Getty Center Dr. exit. Parking $7.00 per vehicle, no reservation required.

EXTRAS Artist-at-work demos, lectures, classes, films. Extensive summer evening series of free concerts and performances often draws a sizeable crowd.

Restaurant at the Getty (310) 440-6810, www.getty.edu. The views, the service, even the silverware—everything but the food is impeccable at this upscale museum restaurant. The chef dishes up creative California/French cuisine that is very good, but not as great as the prices suggest. The best solution? Come at sunset for the delicious cheese plate and a glass of wine.

HIGHLIGHTS

Hans Holbein the Younger's *An Allegory of Passion*

Vincent Van Gogh's *Irises*

***Les Grotsques* tapestries from Beauvais**

The road from J. Paul Getty's billion-dollar museum bequest to architect Richard Meier's billion-dollar building was a long and bitter one. First, a motley network of Getty heirs disputed the oil magnate's will: he had left the bulk of his fortune to the original Getty Museum, an ersatz Roman villa in Malibu (this showcase of Greek, Roman and Etruscan art is currently being renovated). After the will was finally settled and Meier signed on to design the current hilltop Getty Center, it took thirteen years to actually get the museum up and running. Parts of the design process

Vincent van Gogh *Irises* (1889)

GETTY CENTER

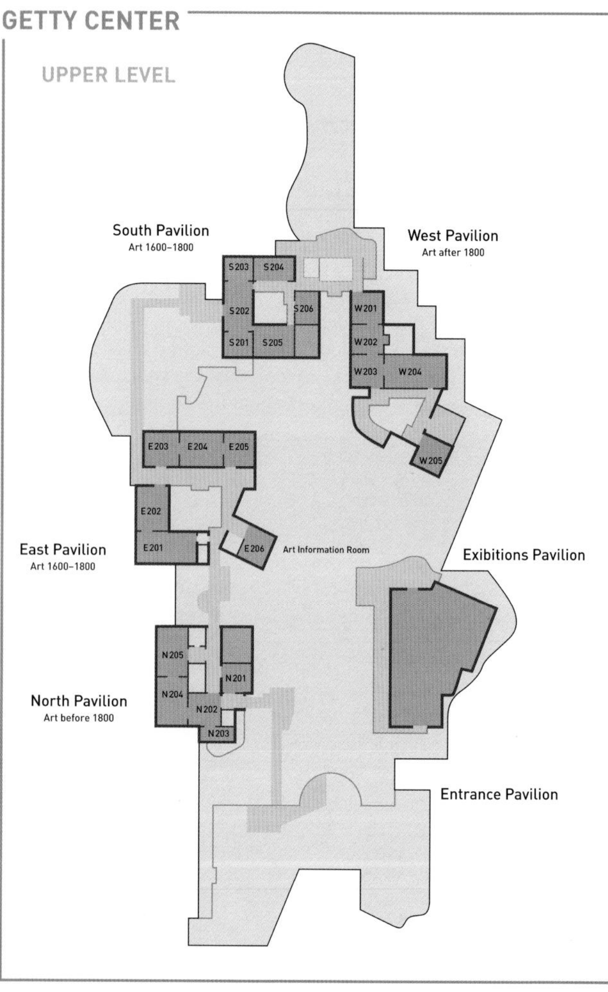

GETTY CENTER

PLAZA LEVEL

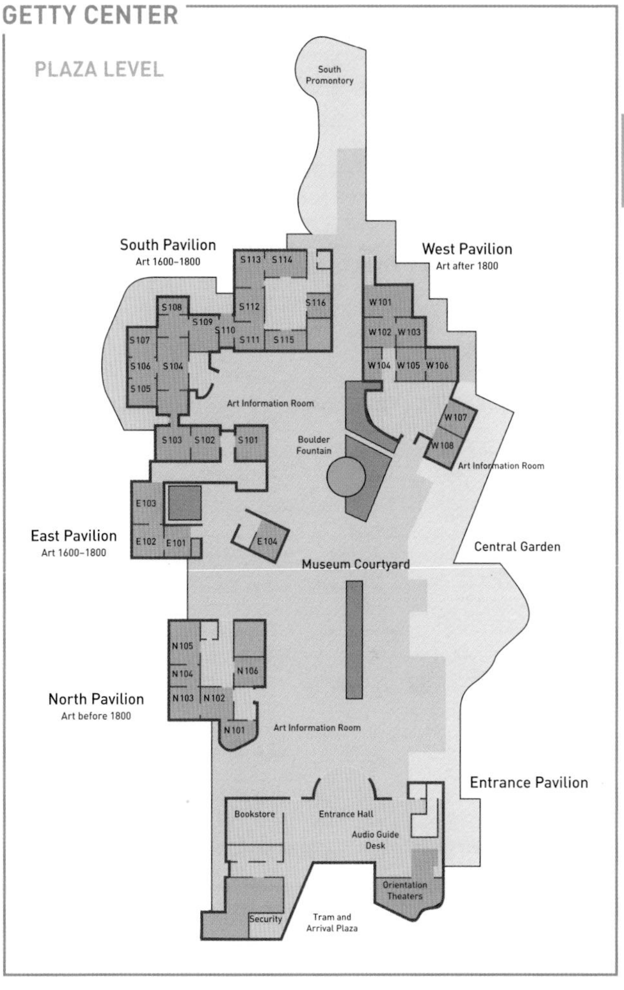

GETTY CENTER

LOWER LEVEL

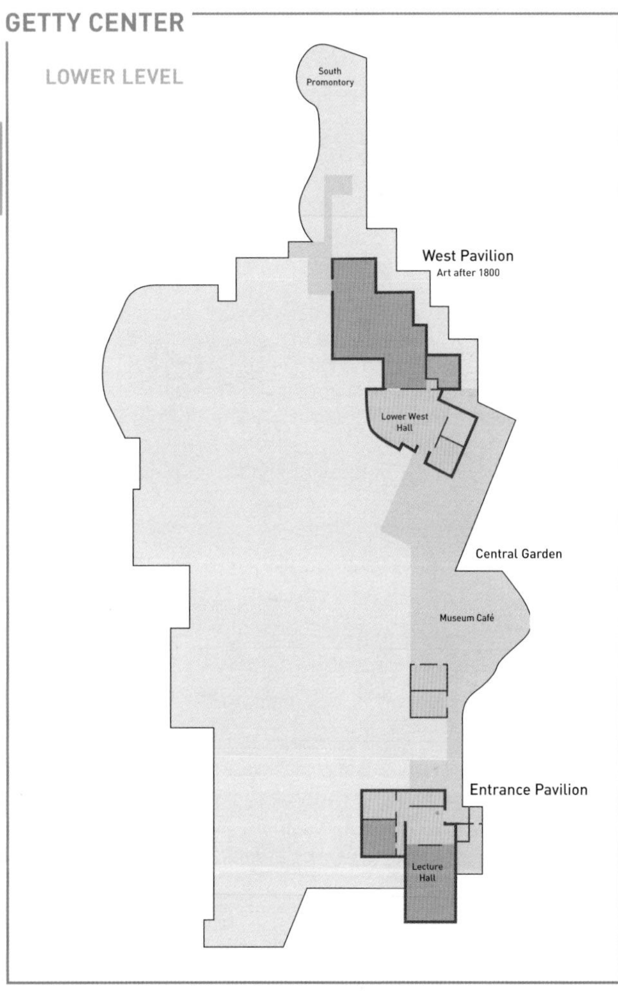

were reportedly as acrimonious as the legal wrangling—the Brentwood Homeowners Association contested the plan at every step, while Meier butted heads with garden designer Robert Irwin and landscape designer Laurie Olin. At the end of that tumultuous path we have the present-day serenity of the Getty complex, which houses the museum and all divisions of the J. Paul Getty Trust, including a research institute and a conservation institute.

THE BUILDING

Tucked high in the Santa Monica Mountains, right on the northern edge of the Los Angeles Basin by the 405 freeway, the Getty Center, with its unparalleled views, has been criticised for lacking urban grit and savvy. However, one of its greatest contributions to the city is the way it calls attention to one of Los Angeles' major attributes—the light. Meier's Bauhaus-influenced International Modernist style is a familiar museum look, but its clean lines and simple forms are elevated by LA's distinctive natural light. Architect Richard Meier's magnificent buildings may look like a stately nuclear power plant from the bottom of the hill, but once you've boarded the gleaming white tram and snaked up the hill to the Arrival Plaza, the cause for admiration becomes in the clear interplay of indoor and outdoor, light and stone. In the end, it is not the collection but the site that keeps people coming back.The buildings are faced in Italian travertine,

ENTIRE GETTY CENTER COMPLEX

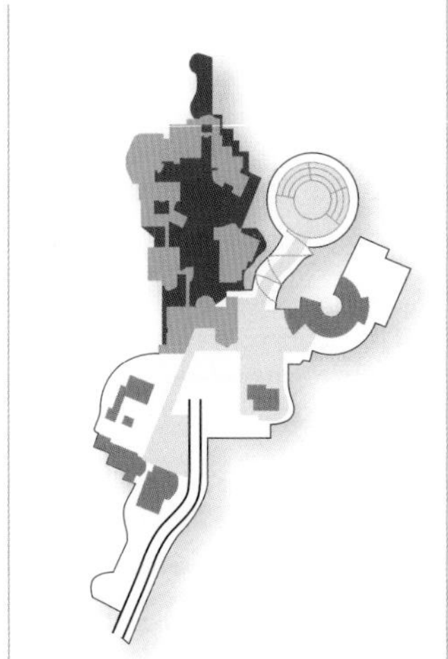

given a rough surface (and, as an unexpected bonus, exposed traces of plant and animal fossils) by a new kind of clad-cutting devised by quarry owner Carlo Mariotti. It was Getty officials who insisted on the use of stone. Meier initially resisted, but was won over by the cut.

Meier wanted to have control of the grounds, envisioning a formal garden to contrast with the modern buildings. Instead, Getty officials chose Robert Irwin, an LA-born artist known for his use of light and natural elements. Irwin had the audacity to modify Meier's building plans, recreating the site's original canyon for his 134,000-square-foot garden bisected by a zigzagging path. Viewed from the high decks of the main building, the garden is beautiful—the landscaped forms are echoed in the maze of red azaleas floating in the central pond. Visitors can also walk through—shielded, on rainy or excessively sunny days, by big umbrellas handed out by museum volunteers.

THE COLLECTIONS

What European art collections owe to royal fiat, American collections owe to industrialists like J. Paul Getty. Born in 1892, Getty inherited an already-successful oil company from his father, and, through shrewd management and daring investments, turned it a multi-billion-dollar giant. By the time he died, in 1976, Getty was one of the richest men in the world.

Though he was an avid art collector, the works shown at his Malibu villa were ridiculed by museums and savvier collectors. When the enormous—estimates put it at $3.5 billion now—Getty Trust was established, museums around the world worried about the competition, and joked that without J. Paul at the helm, the Getty might finally establish a real collection.

And the Trust is pursuing an aggressive acquisition policy. What the collection currently lacks in masterworks, it makes up for in sheer quantity. Even though most of the sizable holdings of Greek, Roman and Etruscan statuary are not on display, there are still too many items to be absorbed in a single visit.

Educating the public about art and about its own holdings remains one of the institution's central missions. Art Information Rooms are scattered throughout the buildings, starting with one on the plaza level of the **NORTH PAVILION**. Titled *Classical Connections*, it draws relationships between ancient art and artefacts and the later works found in the museum. For example, the tableau in **Sebastiano Ricci**'s *Perseus Confronting Phineus with the Head of Medusa* (1705) is shown to echo the scene on a vessel made in Athens in 470 BC, of Orestes stabbing Aegisthus to avenge the murder of his father, Agamemnon.

The plaza level of the North Pavilion is also where you'll find the changing exhibitions of *illuminated manuscripts*, one of the areas where the Getty does have a noted collection. On the upper level, to the left as you exit the elevators, is a collection of *Italian Painting from 1500–1600*. **Lorenzo Cotto** gives us an interesting view of patronage in his *Madonna and Child* (1525-1530), which also shows two obviously wealthy donors kneeling before the holy pair. Baby Jesus bears a marked resemblance to the female donor, and Cotto has depicted the two gazing at each other reverently. **Titian**'s *Portrait of Alfonse d'Avalos, Marchese del Vasto, in Armor with a Page* (1533), a portrait of a military commander and patron of the arts, is one of the Getty's new acquisitions. Don't miss the gallery card explaining the mystery behind **Carpaccio**'s *Hunting on the Lagoon,* an early example of trompe l'oeil with a few unconventional elements that long puzzled art historians.

In *European Paintings from 1400–1500* there is a small room of Northern European paintings with a striking work from **Hans Holbein the Younger**. To create his *Allegory of Passion*, Holbein painted a rearing white horse bearing an intense young rider. With its diamond-shaped exterior frame and lozenge-shaped interior frame, and an inscription from Petrarch's *Conzoniere* ('*E Cosi Desio Me Mena*'—'And So Desire Carries Me Along'), it feels startlingly contemporary.

Many works in *Italian Paintings from 1300–1400* were once parts of altarpieces—one unusual example is the *Chiarito Tabernacle*, created by **Pacino di Bonaguido** in the 1340s. It depicts the communion of the Apostles and was made in *gesso*, a carved plaster technique, then gilded, making it look almost like tooled leather.

An upper level walkway to the **EAST PAVILION** presents the visitor with gorgeous views of the surrounding hills and a bench situated for prime viewing. Once you enter, you're greeted by a *Portrait of John Chetwynd Talbot* (1773), painted by **Pampeo Batoni**. In an early form of the tourist trap, Batoni made a small fortune painting flattering portraits of the rich British on their Grand Tours. Here the subject is in an idealised Roman setting with an adoring spaniel at his feet and the Ludovisi Mars and the Medici Vase at arms length.

Nearby is another Art Information Room that presents an inviting place to play. Children are provided with paper, pencils and still life elements so that they can have a crack at creating some art themselves.

Don't forget to glance up as you enter the *European Paintings from 1600–1700* gallery. **Gerrit van Honthorst**'s *A Musical Group on a Balcony* (1622) will be smiling down—look for the parrot, too. Inside van Honthorst creates a decidedly different scene in *Christ Crowned with Thorns* (1620). In a work influenced by Caravaggio, a downcast Christ painted in chiaroscuro has a crown of thorns forced on his head as a crowd of infidels mock him by torchlight.

In *French and Flemish Paintings from 1600-1700* there is a joint painting by **Peter Paul Rubens** and **Hans Brueghel the Elder**. An allegory of love, *The Return from War: Mars Disarmed by Venus* (1610-1612) shows cupids untying Mars' shoes and scurrying away with his shield and sword. Rubens painted the figures while Brueghel composed the scene and filled in the background.

Dutch and Flemish Paintings from 1600-1725 ushers in a different sensibility. Gone are the sweeping allegorical scenes and tortured Biblical moments; Dutch and Flemish artists were painting for a new class of manufacturers and merchants, milder and more bourgeois in their tastes. This room has lots of landscapes and earthy everyday scenes like **Pieter de Hooch**'s *A Woman Preparing Bread and Butter for a Boy* (1660). In *Rembrandt and His Circle from 1600–1700*, the Getty explores **Rembrandt**'s development and the ways it influenced his contemporaries. There is work here from **Jan Lievens**, a rival of Rembrandt's, his teacher **Pieter Lastman** and student **Gerrit Don Aert de Gelder**.

The plaza level of the **SOUTH PAVILION** opens with a *Making of Furniture* display, showing a step-by-step reconstruction of an oak-veneered writing and toilette table by Francois Oeben, Parisian court carpenter. From there we're plunged into two ornate Louis XIV rooms hung with **tapestries from Beauvais** called *Les Grotesques* (1690-1730). This begins the tour of Getty's collection of decorative arts, arguably the strongest concentration in the permanent holdings. In *French and German Decorative Arts from 1720–1760* look for the Planisphere clock, a mind-boggling piece of mechanics that is able to chart the times of eclipses of Io, one of Jupiter's moons, while simultaneously giving local times around the world. (*La Californie* is carefully painted on a dial.)

The *French Rococo from 1730–1745* rooms show a recreation of a formal salon. The French fondness for collecting Chinese ceramics is demonstrated by the display of a lidded Yong Zheng vase and a Kangxi era inkstand, with a Baumhauer table owned in 1745 by the Russian Czarina Elizabeth. Past a window with a long view of Century City in the foreground and Downtown LA in the back, there are two beds that are always popular with visitors: the *Lit à la Turque*, an enormous pink Turkish bed made by one of the Tilliards, and the *Lit à la Polonaise*, a canopied blue confection crowned by four fluffy tufts of white ostrich feathers.

The most famous Getty-owned painting is **Vincent Van Gogh**'s *Irises* (see picture on p. 49), which the museum bought for the unheard-of price of $53.9 million dollars in 1987. In *European Painting from 1860–1900*, along with the van Gogh are works from **Manet**, **Pissarro** and **Sisley**, and *Portal of Rouen Cathedral in Morning Light* (1894) by **Claude Monet**. From 1892–1894, he painted thirty views of the cathedral at various points throughout the day, using the building to study the effects of light. In this one the cathedral almost fades away in the ghostly glow of morning—it's a refreshing look at Monet that inspires renewed appreciation of the artist.

Two decades ago the Getty began collecting **photographs** and has since amassed a significant body of images. Besides works by

19th-C masters like **Julia Margaret Cameron** and **Carleton Watkins** (whose nature photos helped lead to the National Park system) and great 20th-C lensmen like **Walker Evans** and **Alfred Stieglitz**, the Getty also has many examples of early photo technologies. There are some excellent stereographs that are occasionally on display, as well as daguerreotypes, lantern slides, photogravures and even Polaroids.

UCLA Hammer Museum

OPEN	UCLA Hammer is open from 11 am–7 pm, Tue, Wed, Fri and Sat; 11 am–9 pm, Thur. Closed Mondays. The museum store is open during regular museum hours.
CHARGES	Regular admission $5; seniors over 65 $3; free for students with ID and children under 17 accompanied by an adult. Admission is free on Thursdays.
GUIDED VISITS	Free docent-led tours of the changing exhibitions every Thursday at 6 pm. Lunchtime 'art-talks' every Wednesday at 12.30 pm, check website for programme. Tours of the entire museum can be arranged for groups of ten or more, scheduled a month in advance (call (310) 443-7041).
DISABLED ACCESS	Fully wheelchair accessible, special parking
SERVICES	Bookstore, café, Grunwald Center Study Room (open by appointment only), sculpture garden
TELEPHONE	(310) 443-7000
WEB	www.hammer.ucla.edu
MAIN ENTRANCE	10899 Wilshire Blvd.
GETTING THERE	By bus: Take the 20, 21, 720, SM1, SM2, SM3, SM8 or SM12. By car: From the 405 freeway, take the Wilshire Blvd. exit. Park in the museum's underground lot ($2.75 for 3 hours with validation).
SERVICES	Fiction and poetry reading series featuring well-known writers. Recent guests have included David Foster Wallace, Jonathan Lethem, Marilynne Robinson and Galway Kinnel. The Hammer Conversations series pairs personalities from the arts.

UCLA HAMMER MUSEUM

Hammer Collection
Daumier
Hammer Collection
Store

GALLERY LEVEL

Courtyard

COURTYARD LEVEL

Parking
Lobby

WILSHIRE LOBBY LEVEL

HIGHLIGHTS

Honore Daumier's *Collection of Bronze Busts*

Andrew Wyeth's *Daydream*

Rembrandt van Rijn's *Juno*

A confidant of Lenin and a collector of Daumier, Armand Hammer was a wealthy industrialist best known as the chairman of Occidental Petroleum, which financed the museum's construction. (Contrary to rumour, Hammer—who died three weeks after the museum opened in 1990—was not named after the ubiquitous Arm & Hammer baking soda, though at one point he did mischievously try to buy the company. However, his father helped start the American Communist Party and might have actually named his son after the Socialist Labour Party's arm-and-hammer device.)

Hammer left a stellar collection of Honoré Daumier's paintings, drawings, sculptures and lithographs, as well as a nice selection of 19th-C French painters, early Old Masters and 18th-20th-C American painters. Since Ann Philbin took over as director in 1999, the museum has built a reputation for contemporary art with its Hammer Projects programme, in which emerging artists create site-specific works in the building's high-ceilinged lobby space.

THE BUILDING

The UCLA Hammer started life as a formal gallery designed to showcase Armand Hammer's distinguished, if unspectacular, collection. Designed by the late Edward Larrabbee Barnes, a New York-based modernist who studied under Bauhaus founder Walter Gropius, the building is a strong grey and white striped block located at the edge of Westwood Village. After Hammer's death in 1990, construction stopped; parts of the building, including a planned 300-seat theatre, remained unfinished.

Currently the museum is planning a major renovation that will add exhibition, lecture and classroom space, as well as a restaurant and a larger bookstore in the courtyard. A new, state-of-the-art theatre is also being built as a home for the renowned UCLA Film and Television Archive screenings. A team of star designers have been brought in to make the museum more open to the street. It is headed by Los Angeles-based architect Michael Maltzman (who designed New York's MoMA Queens), graphic designer Bruce Mau and interiors doyenne Petra Blaisse.

THE COLLECTION

Entering the museum can be disorienting. You park in an underground lot, ride up an elevator and step into an echoing, marbled lobby that could be the corporate headquarters of a financial consulting firm. Until, of course, you realise that right above the lone security guard, an entire wall has been taken over by a stunning, sprawling art installation. Hammer Projects change every few months, but there are generally at least two new artists on display at any one time—in the lobby and in an enclosed gallery off the lobby space.

One flight up from the lobby level is a serene courtyard shielded from the street, a popular lunch spot for local office workers. *Gallery 6*, the museum's lecture hall, is also on this level. On the next floor are the galleries, bookstore and administrative offices.

The curators have done a good job of enlivening the permanent collection with *Writings on the Wall*. This is an installation of personal views on specific paintings by well-known and famous art lovers, including **Steve Martin**, **Diane Keaton**, **Ricky Jay**, actor and multimedia artist **Martin Mull**, artist **Mary Woronov** and tape and media installation artist **Bruce Yonemoto**. Mull, who chooses **Vincent Van Gogh**'s *Hospital at Saint-Remy*, makes a passionate argument for forgetting about van Gogh's mental state; Keaton's commentary on a portrait of a young girl by **Jean-Baptiste Camille Corot** perhaps reveals more about herself and her relationship with her daughter; Martin equivocates over whether **Andrew**

Wyeth's *Daydream*—a nude portrait of his longtime model Helga Testorf taking an afternoon nap under a mosquito net—is actually any good.

The Hammer Collection includes one of **Gilbert Stuart**'s many portraits of George Washington. Painted in 1822, it shows the general—delicate hands folded, mouth firmly set—posed in front of a rainbow. Also in the collection is **Henri de Toulouse-Lautrec**'s *Tonc, Seated on a Table* (1879-1881). Known for his showgirls, dancers, circus scenes and theatre posters, Toulouse-Lautrec also loved to paint dogs; this one is particularly endearing and a bit out of place amidst the grander paintings, like **John Singer Sargent**'s *Dr. Pozzi at Home* (1881). A full-length portrait of the Parisian art collector and gynaecologist in a dramatic red dressing gown over a ruffled white shirt, it is one of the few portraits of the time that take the sitter out of a formal setting. The museum's old masters are presided over by **Rembrandt van Rijn**'s majestic *Juno* (1662-65).

THE DAUMIER COLLECTION

French satirist **Honoré Daumier**'s cartoons and caricatures, with their expressive lines and humorous captions, draw a lively and tumultuous portrait of French life—political, social and domestic—in the 19th C. Between 1970 and 1990, Armand Hammer amassed over 7,500 pieces of Daumier's work, the bulk which came from his acquisition of George Longstreet and Hans Rothe's exemplary collections.

The museum displays this trove of irascible politicians, henpecked husbands, flirtatious maidens and outraged wives in an ongoing series of themed exhibitions. One particularly good specimen, *Cupid* (1853), depicts the cherub as a leering old man with wiry legs, wearing a flower garland and a tutu, squinting through a monocle and puffing a cigarette. However, the highlight of the collection is the scowling gallery of bronze busts of friends and members of Parliament.

TEMPORARY EXHIBITIONS

Across the courtyard are four temporary galleries. The latest, and most impressive, exhibition was a retrospective of the reclusive

Lee Bontecou, one of the few women to make an impression on the male-dominated, New York-centric, American art world of the 1960s and 1970s; Bontecou has spent the past thirty years out of the public eye, rarely showing her work. The Hammer's success in persuading her to open up the barn where she had been storing her new work over the decades was seen as a major coup, and the resulting exhibition—which gathered 70 sculptures and 80 drawings from Bontecou's own holdings and from private and public collections—was the critical success of the year.

ARCHITECTS IN LOS ANGELES: JOHN LAUTNER AND THE BIRTH OF THE GOOGIE

Odds are you've seen a Lautner house before, most likely the Elrod Residence in whose swimming pool James Bond gets thrashed by Bunny and Thumper in *Diamonds are Forever*. Or perhaps you've seen Lautner's sleek Chemosphere as the ultimate bachelor pad in Brian de Palma's *Body Double*. But chances are you don't know Lautner's name. John Lautner was full of contradictions—a lesser-known architect whose houses became icons, the quintessential LA architect who didn't even like LA—but his work, taken together, forms a tremendous range of experimentation and had a measurable impact on the architecture of California.

Unlike most LA mid-century moderns, who used orthogonal plans, window grids, and post-and-beam construction, Lautner built structural systems (from wood beams to steel trusses, from cables to concrete shells) in organic ellipses, trapezoids and triangles, with every building intimately tied to its site. Lautner's work is evocative of LA itself—the terrain of mountains and beaches, the swooping freeways and emerging car culture—but he never liked the city. He also repudiated the fantastical-seeming elements of his design; what appeared to the public like flying saucers and crazy shapes were to Lautner the most rational responses to site and programme. This rational characteristic of form tied to space led to the creation of a whole mode of design with his Googie coffeeshop, built in the early 1949—since then, the upswept roofs, jutting angles and boomerang arches of a whole generation of bowling alleys and restaurants have been designated 'Googie' architecture.

LAUTNER IN LA

Chemosphere 776 Torreyson Drive, West Hollywood. Visible from Mulholland Drive.

Sheets L'Horizon Apartments 10901 W. Strathmore Drive. Mostly inhabited by UCLA students; you can wander around inside the complex.

Wolff House 8530 Hedges Place

Silvertop 2138 Micheltorena St.

Lautner House 2007 Micheltorena St.

in the area

BEVERLY HILLS & WESTWOOD

Greystone Mansion and Gardens 905 Loma Vista Dr., (310) 550-4796. In 1928, oil magnate Edward Doheny built this mansion for his son, who was murdered by his secretary three weeks after moving in. The house is still used for special events and occasional concerts, and the grounds are open to the public, free of charge. With panoramic views of the city, this is a good place for a quiet picnic. **Map p. 44, 3A**

Museum of Television and Radio

Museum of Television and Radio 465 N. Beverly Drive, (310) 786-1000, (310) 786-1025 (schedule of daily events), www.mtr.org. The past and present of television and radio. Events are the main draw—daily screenings, radio broadcasts, and best of all, lively panels with casts and crews of popular television shows like *West Wing* and *The Daily Show*. **Map p. 44, 3C**

Museum of Tolerance 9786 W. Pico Blvd., (310) 553-8403, www.museumoftolerance.com. This hands-on museum grew out of the Simon Wiesenthal Center, dedicated to educating people about the Holocaust. The museum hosts a series of interactive exhibits that explore our reactions to intolerance, including the American civil rights movement and modern-day crises in Bosnia and Rwanda. Occasionally feels a bit like a theme park, but is generally well-done and thought-provoking. **Off map**

Skirball Cultural Center & Museum 2701 N. Sepulveda Blvd., (310) 440-4500, www.skirball.org. Up the hill from the Getty Center is this Jewish cultural institution designed by architect Moishe Safdie, hosting changing exhibitions on Jewish life in America.

Frequent film screenings, readings, concerts and talks, plus performances by LA Theatre Works. Also has a kosher restaurant, Zeidler's. **Off map**

UCLA Fowler Museum of Cultural History UCLA campus, off Hilgard, (310) 825-4361, www.fmch.ucla.edu. Impressive shows approach unexpected topics—the history of the botanica, Haitian voodoo flags—from many angles. Also has a world-class collection of ethnographic and archaeological objects, most donated by noted collectors. Recent emphasis on Latino topics. **Map p. 45, 4C**

SANTA MONICA, VENICE & CULVER CITY

Beyond Baroque 681 Venice Blvd., (310) 822-3006, www.beyondbaroque.com. A mainstay of the Westside literary community, Beyond Baroque has been hosting readings and performances since 1969. Tom Waits, Mary Gaitskill, Raymond Carver, Allen Ginsberg have all read here, Viggo Mortensen is a long-time supporter and current trustee. Free writing workshops in poetry, fiction, creative non-fiction are open to all. **Off map**

Camera Obscura 1450 Ocean Ave., Santa Monica (310) 394-1227. When it's time to get out of the sun, stop by the senior citizens' home and ask for the key to the camera obscura, a dark room with a flat white disc where street scenes are projected by lens and mirror. Built over a century ago, it was once a popular attraction for beach-going visitors, but is now rarely visited. **Map p. 42, 3D**

Center for Land Use and Interpretation 9331 Venice Blvd., (310) 839-5722, www.clui.org. A research institution dedicated to understanding our impact on the landscape, the centre digs into culture, history and sociology. Runs popular bus tours where director Matthew Coolidge's humour elevates deliberately dry subjects like the gravel pits of Irwindale. Also maintains a searchable nationwide database that allows you to find, say, nuclear or radioactive sites in Alaska. **Map p. 46, 1C**

Edgemar Center for the Arts 2437 Main St., (310) 399-3666, www.edgemar.org. A rehearsal and performance space for theatre, dance, art and film. Housed in a Frank Gehry building that also provides space for the MOCA store (see p. 11) and Rockenwagner restaurant. **Map p. 43, 1D**

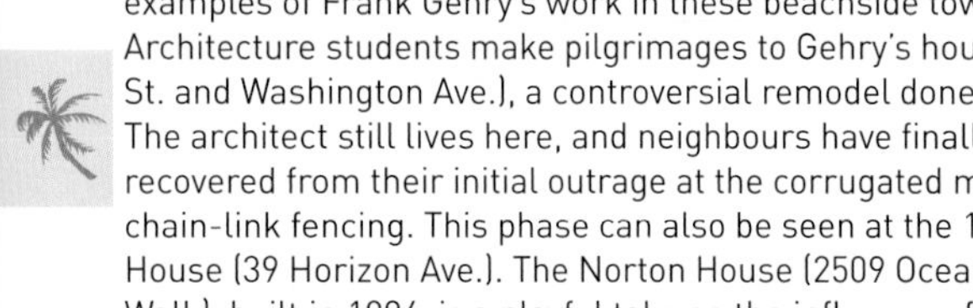

Gehry buildings Besides the Edgemar, there are many pre-Bilbao examples of Frank Gehry's work in these beachside towns. Architecture students make pilgrimages to Gehry's house (22nd St. and Washington Ave.), a controversial remodel done in 1978. The architect still lives here, and neighbours have finally recovered from their initial outrage at the corrugated metal and chain-link fencing. This phase can also be seen at the 1980 Spiller House (39 Horizon Ave.). The Norton House (2509 Ocean Front Walk), built in 1984, is a playful take on the influence of Japanese design. The former TBWA Chiat Day headquarters (340 Main St.) is unmistakable—just look for the enormous pair of Claes Oldenburg binoculars. **Map p. 43, 2D**

Museum of Jurassic Technology 9341 Venice Blvd., Culver City, (310) 836-6131, www.mtj.org. This hushed institution is one man's eccentric work of genius; nothing here is real, but nothing is quite fake, either. It is full of the pseudo-scientific and quasi-historical, with lovingly constructed exhibits about bats that fly through walls, women with horns and the convoluted bylaws of forgotten civilisations. If you need a dose of prosaic reality, end your visit with lunch at the In-N-Out burger stand, right next door. **Map p. 46, 1C**

Santa Monica Museum of Art 2525 Michigan Ave., Space G-5, (310) 586-6488, www.smmoa.org. Moving into Bergamot Station gave the Santa Monica Museum of Art a jolt of much-needed energy, and now the compact institution stages shows like the recent Black Belt, examining the connection between African-American and Asian-American culture in the 1970s with commissioned work that ranged from watercolours to a motion-sensor sound chamber. **Map p. 42, 3A**

Carl Cheng's *Walk on LA*

Singing Beach Chairs The beach at Gold St. Between the Venice Boardwalk and the Santa Monica Pier there's a stretch of surf that's perfect for boogie boarding, and a pair of pastel beach chairs that sing when the wind is blowing, thanks to the aluminium pipes that artist Doug Hollis fitted into the backs. **Map p. 42, 3D**

Star ECO Station 10101 W. Jefferson Blvd., Culver City, (310) 842-8060, www.ecostation.org. For a much more intimate zoo experience, visit this 'last chance' stop for exotic wildlife like carpet pythons, Savannah monitors and flap-necked chameleons. Run by the Bozzi family and their network of volunteers, this eco attraction also offers an environmental education centre with a series of hands-on exhibits exploring various natural habitats. Only open at weekends. **Off map**

Walk on LA at the Santa Monica Pier On the sand north of the Santa Monica pier is artist Carl Cheng's 1988 sculpture, a functioning concrete roller imprinted with a real cityscape. It occasionally gets rolled along the sand so that beach-goers can stomp on a mini-LA. **Map p. 42, 3D**

Venice Canals Between Washington Blvd. and Venice Blvd. At the turn of the 19th C, Abbot Kinney envisioned Venice as a city of canals modelled after Venice, Italy. Much of the original 16 miles of canal were paved over, but in the 1960s some people (including Jim Morrison) began moving back into the area and restoring the homes. Today there is still a fairy-tale neighbourhood of working canals lined with upscale houses. Look out for locals boating to the Baja Cantina for margaritas. **Map p. 43, 4D**

commercial galleries

Bergamot Station in sunny Santa Monica and a slew of new spaces in deceptively cool Culver City are your best bets for exciting contemporary artists. Yes, they're a drive from the Getty and the Hammer, but once you get there you'll find walk-friendly streets and a wealth of new works.

Allen Pearce 1225 Abbot Kinney Blvd., (310) 399-0040, www.allenpearce.com. Primarily a gallery of owner/sculptor Alma Allen's elegant yet elemental carvings, bowls and furniture. Also shows feltmaker Kelly Muloy and a very artistic dog named Fritz. **Map p. 43, 3D** ❶

BERGAMOT STATION

2525 Michigan Ave., Santa Monica, (310) 829-5854. Over 30 quality galleries are clustered together in this converted train station depot—once home to the Red Line Trolley. Occasional art auctions in the summer months, great Gallery Café for homemade soups, creative sandwiches and fresh salads. **Map p. 42, 3A** ❷

Frank Lloyd Space B-5, (310) 264-3866, www.franklloyd.com. Dedicated to contemporary ceramics artists.

Frumkin/Duval Gallery Space T-1, (310) 453-1850, www.frumkinduvalgallery.com. Provocative exhibitions by emerging young artists around the world—including from Yugoslavia, China, Israel.

Patricia Correia Space E-2, (310) 264-1760, www.correia gallery.com. Focus on contemporary Mexican-American and Chicano/Chicana artists. Also has a press.

Peter Fetterman Space A-7, (310) 453-6463, www.peter fetterman.com. 19th- and 20th-C photography. Henri Cartier Bresson, Robert Capa, Alfred Eisenstadt, extensive inventory of familiar photos in sports, classic Hollywood, fashion and photojournalism.

Shoshana Wayne Space B-1 (310) 453-7535, www.shosana wayne.com. Paintings, sculptures, installations from emerging and mid-career artists. The gallery has done several shows of Yoko Ono's work.

Track 16 Space C-1, (310) 264-4678, www.track16.com. Art as cultural commentary—especially strong on graphic artists. Also an event space with a huge collection of vintage signs, and a reading/film/performance series, Track 16 Nights.

BLK/MRKT Gallery 6009 Washington Blvd., Culver City, (310) 837-1989, www.blkmrktgallery.com. Emphasis on urban contemporary artists, influenced by world of skaters, graffiti artists. **Map p. 46, 1-2A** 3

Blum and Poe 2754 S. La Cienega Blvd., Culver City, (310) 836-2062, www.blumandpoe.com. One of the first galleries to move to Culver City, shows rising art stars like Sam Durant, Dave Muller, Takashi Murakami, Yoshitomo Nara. **Map p. 46, 1-2A** 3

Cherry de los Reyes 12611 Venice Blvd., Culver City, (310)398-7404, www.cherrydelosreyes.com. Young gallerist Mary Cherry started putting on shows in her garage, has since moved on to this spare space. Paintings, installations, mixed-media from experimental young artists. **Off map p. 43, 4A** 5

Christopher Grimes 916 Colorado Ave., Santa Monica, (310) 587-3373, www.cgrimes.com. Modern and contemporary paintings, sculpture, photography, mixed-media installations and works on paper. Local and international artists—Anthony Hernandez, Allan Sekula. **Map p. 42, 3C** 6

Gagosian 456 N. Camden Dr., Beverly Hills, (310) 271-9400, www.gagosian.com. Blockbuster gallerist Larry Gagosian actually opened his first space in Los Angeles, but most of his notoriety comes from big ticket sales in New York. The Beverly Hills gallery has recently shown Vanessa Beecroft and Helmut Newton, but functions more as a retail outlet for prints. **Map p. 44, 3D** ❼

GR2 2062 Sawtelle Blvd., (310) 445-9276, www.gr2.net. The Giant Robot store's gallery off-shoot shows indie artists like kozyndan, Souther Salazar, David Choe and Saelee Oh. **Off map p. 45, 1D** ❽

LA Louver 45 North Venice Blvd., Venice, (310) 822-4955, www.lalouver.com. Wide ranging shows of contemporary artists. From the well-known—David Hockney, Ed Moses—to the up-and-coming. **Map p. 43, 4D** ❾

Lizabeth Oliveria 2712 S. La Cienega Blvd., Culver City, (310) 837-1073, www.lizabetholiveria.com. Contemporary painting and photography from this San Francisco transplant. **Map p. 46, 1A** ❿

Sandroni Rey 2762 S. La Cienega Blvd, Culver City, (310) 280-0111, www.sandronirey.com. Next door to Blum & Poe, often shows contemporary German artists. **Map p. 46, 1A** ❹

Spencer Jon Helfen 9200 W. Olympic Blvd., (310) 273-8838, www.helfenfinearts.com. Paintings and sculpture by California modernists with a focus on artists from the 1930s. **Map p. 44, 4D** ⓫

Susanne Vielmetter Los Angeles Projects 5797 W. Washington Blvd., (323) 933-2117, www.vielmetter.com. A large, appealing space, showing new works by well-reviewed artists like Wamgechi Mutu and Tam Van Tran. **Map p. 46, 2A** ⓬

eat

BEVERLY HILLS & WESTWOOD

$ **Diddy Riese Cookies** 926 Broxton Ave. [Le Conte Ave.], (310) 208-0448. Hungry UCLA students and nostalgic alums crowd this Westwood Village storefront, prepared to wait in line for what might be the best deal in LA—two fresh-baked cookies sandwiched together by a scoop of ice cream, for a mere dollar.

The Fountain Coffee Shop at the Beverly Hills Hotel

The ice cream is nothing special (they use Dreyer's, a mid-range supermarket brand) but those cookies are warm, gooey and delicious—try the candy cookie. **Map p. 45, 3C** ❶

In-N-Out 922 Gayley Ave. [Weyburn Ave.], (800) 786-1000, www.in-n-out.com. Southern Californians are born loving these burgers. The menu is simple—burgers, fries and shakes—and the family-owned chain's obsession with freshness makes this the anti-McDonalds. As does the secret menu ('animal style' means grilled with mustard and topped with sautéed onions). This eye-catching outlet, done in their signature bright red and yellow, was designed by LA-based Kanner Architects. **Map p. 45, 2C** ❷

$$ **Fountain Coffee Shop** 9641 Sunset Blvd., (310) 276-2251 Located in the very pink Beverly Hills Hotel—whose decor is both super swanky and extravagantly bad in a way that only Beverly Hills can do—this is the low-cost excuse to spend time on the grounds of the storied hotel. A classic soda fountain with pink bar stools, this is where the Guns N' Roses were signed, and Lucille Ball was a regular. **Map p. 44, 2B** ❸

Kate Mantilini 9101 Wilshire Blvd , (310) 278-3699. This is older Hollywood's late-night canteen—open till midnight during the week and 2 am on weekends. High-powered agents and their higher-powered clients nosh on classic American food with an upscale twist. The sleek glass and steel building was designed by LA-based architecture firm Morphosis, which also designed the controversial new CalTrans building downtown. **Map p. 44, 4D** ❹

Nate 'n' Al 414 N. Beverly Dr. [Brighton Way], (310) 274-0101. If you're a loyal Larry King fan, breakfast at this back-to-basics deli that's been a Beverly Hills staple for years may be the best place to spot him—he's reportedly such a devoted customer that he bought a house close by. Moist, flavourful pastrami on fresh rye bread is a runaway favourite. **Map p. 44, 3C** ❺

Shaherzad 1422 Westwood Blvd., (310) 474-1700. Los Angeles' sizeable Persian community frequents this warm, welcoming spot. A strange mix of formal and casual, the restaurant features a wood-fired circular oven where a busy baker constantly turns out fresh flatbread. Also good are lamb kebabs and well-spiced stews. **Map p. 45, 2D** ❻

$$$$ **Mr. Chow's** 344 N Camden Dr, (310) 278-9911. Nobody asks for the menu at this inexplicably hot Chinese restaurant that's a

Hal's Bar and Grill

constant favourite of any celebrity who has ever walked a red carpet. Tell the waiter what you like—think standard Chinese fare—and he'll bring out the chef's 'choice'. If you go, don't go for the food. It's the ridiculously star-studded surroundings (try Wednesday night) and the only-in-LA experience that will keep you from fainting when you see the bill. **Map p. 44, 3D** ⑦

SANTA MONICA, VENICE & CULVER CITY

$ **Abbot's Habit** 1401 Abbot Kinney Blvd., (310) 399-1171. A funky coffeehouse that draws a complete cross-section of Venice's diverse population—the locals love it so much that it feels like a neighbourhood club. Strong, strong coffee. **Map p. 43, 4C-D** ⑧

La Dijonaise 8703 Washington Blvd., Culver City, (310) 287-2770, www.ladijonaise.com. This popular French café and boulangerie is a bustling, sunlit spot that quickly fills up with studio suits—Sony's offices are right around the corner—and employees of the adjacent complex of furniture showrooms. Located in the renovated Helm's Bakery, a historic building that churned out loaves of bread until the 1960s, La Dijonaise still has delicious croissants and baguettes, plus main courses off standard French menus, accompanied by crispy fries. **Map p. 46, 1B** ⑨

Omelette Parlor 2732 Main St, (310) 399-7892. With a friendly neighbourhood vibe and hearty servings, this is a good place to fuel up for a day at the galleries or shopping on Abbot Kinney. Best seats are in the rear garden. If you're up extra early, omelettes are half price. **Map p. 43, 1D** ⑩

Santa Monica Farmers Market Arizona Ave. & 2nd St. [off the 3rd St. Promenade], (310) 458-8712. On Wednesday (9 am–2 pm) foodies, locals and tourists flock to this abundant market. Long a favourite of well-known chefs like Mark Peel of Campanile and Evan Kleinman of Angeli Café (who also hosts KCRW's Good Eats radio show), you'll find heirloom produce aplenty, as well as a whole row of cooked food stalls. There's also a popular Sunday market (9:30 am–1pm) on Main St. between Hill and Ocean Park. **Map p. 42, 2D** ⑪

$$ **Jin Patisserie** 1202 Abbot Kinney, (310) 399-8801. A serene little Venice hideaway where pastry chef Kristy Choo, who trained at the Raffles Hotel in Singapore, serves up a beautifully plated afternoon tea. Sit in the secluded garden courtyard and taste an

assortment of scones, tea sandwiches, pastries and petit fours, accompanied by a carefully brewed pot of tea. Cakes, pastries and chocolates are also sold at the counter. **Map p. 43, 3D** ⓬

Hide Sushi 2040 Sawtelle Blvd., (310) 477-7242. Across the street from the Giant Robot store/gallery, this stretch of Sawtelle is packed with Japanese restaurants. Hide (pronounced 'hee-day') feels like an authentic Tokyo neighbourhood sushi spot with its rough wooden tables and gruff but good-natured service. The sushi is outstanding—every slab of fish tastes like it was just snatched from the sea. Especially good is the albacore. No reservations, be prepared for a wait. **Off map p. 42, 3A** ⓭

Library Alehouse 2911 Main St., (310) 314-4855, www.libraryalehouse.com. A long, wood-panelled room that leads out to a pretty back garden, this cosy restaurant/bar lives up to its name with 25 beers, ciders and ales from Northern California's best breweries on draught (even root beer on tap!). The food is just as good—favourites include the Ahi burger, served rare with searing wasabi coleslaw. **Map p. 43, 2D** ⓮

$$$ **Amuse Café** 796 Main Street, (310) 450-1956, www.amusecafe.com. Precocious star chef Brooke Williamson isn't even thirty, but she's already spent nearly a decade in some of LA's best kitchens; this is her first venture as co-owner, and it's a winner. Located in a cheerful two-story yellow bungalow, you can opt to sit in the herb-filled garden. Dishes are reasonably priced and all market-fresh, and, of course, every meal begins with an amuse bouche. **Map p. 43, 3D** ⓯

Hal's Bar and Grill 1349 Abbot Kinney Blvd., (310) 396-3105. The gathering place of choice for many of Venice's clubby 35-and-up art crowd, including some of the artists whose work lines the restaurant's walls. Evenings can get raucous here as the Caesar salads get eaten up and the cantaloupe martinis keep on flowing. **Map p. 43, 4D** ⓰

Primitivo Wine Bar 1025 Abbot Kinney Blvd, (310) 396-5353, www.primitivowinebistro.com. A festive spot filled with groups of stylish Venice locals sharing wine and plates of Mediterranean/Californian tapas. Standout dishes include the braised short ribs and spicy shrimp, though portions tend to be on the small side. Wine list heavy on Spanish labels, many available by the half glass. **Map p. 43, 3D** ⓱

BARS

Boe at the Crescent 403 N Crescent Dr. (310) 247-0505. A recent redesign has turned this tiny hotel restaurant into a hip lounge that's a much-needed addition to the local scene. Sit on the front patio, twinkling with tea lights, or settle down beside the crackling fire. **Map p. 44, 3C** 18

Whist at the Viceroy 1819 Ocean Ave., 310 260 7500, www.viceroysantamonica.com. Hollywood Regency gets reimagined by designer Kelly Wearstler (who also did the Avalon). Always packed with tables of pretty Europeans on holiday and the LA Westsiders that love them. The restaurant turns into a table-hopping party as the night wears on. Poolside cabanas available. **Map p. 42, 4D** 19

ARCHITECTS IN LOS ANGELES: FRANK LLOYD WRIGHT

It was Frank Lloyd Wright's personality more than his actual buildings that changed the architectural landscape of Los Angeles. With his belief in the importance of nature and 'the destruction of the box' in favour of a composition of spaces, Wright gained the admiration of a whole generation of new architects—his students and disciples included R.M. Schindler and Richard Neutra (see box on p. 103), both Austrian emigrants of the 1920s who worked for Wright briefly, and later on, John Lautner (see p. 63). All three came to LA both to get away from Wright's overbearing presence and to oversee the creation of Wright buildings.

Wright's signature work in Los Angeles was his (short-lived) experimentation with concrete textile blocks influenced by Mayan architecture. The blocks formed a monumentality that was at odds with both the local vernacular of stucco and lightweight construction, and with the climate (all of these houses have required extensive restoration). In spite of Wright's focus on organic architecture, his houses did not respond to either the variations of LA terrain or the characteristic freedom

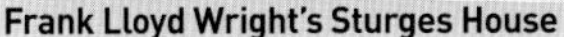

Frank Lloyd Wright's Sturges House

of space in the way that the architecture of Schindler, Neutra, and Lautner would do.

Hollyhock House at Barnsdall Park 4808 Hollywood Blvd. The house itself is closed for restoration, but the grounds are accessible. **Map p. 87, 4B**

Anderton Court Shops 333 Rodeo Dr. Open during business hours. **Map p. 44, 4D**

La Miniatura (Millard House) 645 Prospect Crescent. **Map p. 122, 1A**

Freeman House 1962 Glencoe Way. **Map p. 87, 1A**

Sturges House 449 Skyeway Road (see picture above). **Off map p. 45, 1B**

shop

SANTA MONICA, VENICE & CULVER CITY

Locals like to make fun of the Third Street Promenade (Map p. 42, 1-2D), with its hordes of high-schoolers and tourists vying for sidewalk space, but this pedestrian shopping street—ruled by a herd of topiary dinosaurs—collects every brand-name chain in one convenient spot. North of the Promenade, on Montana Ave., new moms with Prada diaper bags shop and lunch; further south is Santa Monica's Main St. Though Main is just blocks from the beach, the vibe is less surfer (go to the Venice boardwalk, which runs parallel, for that) and more farmers market chic. Radiating out from Main is Abbot Kinney, the new heart of artsy Venice.

BOOKS & FILM

Cinefile 11280 Santa Monica Blvd., (310) 312-8836, www.cinefilevideo.com. Maybe everything should be classified under the Cinefile system, which departs from the typical Action, Comedy, Horror categories and files films under headings like Military Training Films. If something's obscure, you'll find it here. Sprawling, haphazard rows and a whiff of film school elitism don't keep this store from being the hands down favourite of local cinephiles. Next door to the Nuart (see Entertainment). **Off map p. 45, 1D** 1

Hennessey + Ingalls 214 Wilshire Blvd., Santa Monica, (310) 458-9074. 10,000 square feet of books on architecture, graphic design, fine art, interior design and more. Enormous collection of monographs, university press publications and rare books. The 50,000 volumes are housed in a spare and calming store designed by Marmol + Radziner. **Map p. 42, 2D** 2

Equator Books 1103 Abbot Kinney Blvd, (310) 399-5510, www.equatorbooks.com. This brand new bookstore/art gallery has been embraced with open arms and pocketbooks by the local arts community—their opening exhibition featured Raymond Pettibon, Billy Al Bengston and Ed Ruscha. Speciality categories include Surf & Skate, Prostitutes & Call Girls and Circus & Freaks. **Map p. 43, 3D** 3

CLOTHES

Brentwood Country Mart 225 26th St., (310) 393-5238. This sprawling red barn houses a low-profile complex of boutiques that draws lots of high-profile local shoppers, including Spielbergs, Schwarzeneggers and Hankses. One of the best stores is **Apartment Number 9**, 310-394-9440. Men need a little style too, and the girls who run this boutique know how to add a touch of frippery without descending into foppery. Selections are definitely fashion-conscious, but won't look out of place on an older gentleman. If browsing and buying makes you hungry, stop for some tasty roast chicken at **Reddi-Chick**. **Off map p. 42, 1A** 4

Last Chance Boutique 8712 Washington Blvd., Culver City, (310) 287-2333. It seems like there's always a Diane von Furstenberg dress on sale somewhere, including this bare-bones chop shop, but Last Chance also has harder-to-find bargains on brands like Catherine Malandrino, Seven jeans and local favourites Mon Petit Oiseau. Most stock from upscale local boutiques—Tracey Ross, Madison, etc. **Map p. 46, 1B** 5

Mademoiselle Pearl 1311 Montana Ave., Santa Monica, (310) 576-7116. Before Jennifer Nicholson (daughter of Jack) started her own clothing line, she was running this high-fashion boutique—Vivienne Westwood and Narciso Rodriguez sold here. Now the store also stocks her well-received line. **Map p. 42, 1C** 6

Papillon 2712 Main St. Santa Monica, (310) 452-0969. Babies who get to shop at Papillon are lucky little sproglets whose parents dress them in the hippest of threads, some with a tongue-in-cheek twist, so that the parents don't feel too grown-up. **Map p. 43, 1D** 7

ZJ Boarding House 2619 Main St., Santa Monica (310) 392-5646, www.zjboarding house.com. Pick up a pair of snowboard boots, a sleek wetsuit or a new set of wheels for your skateboard at this well-stocked shop. Almost all of the staff hit the surf, street or snow regularly, which means that they have real-life advice on the type of gear you should buy. If you're into the look but are more comfortable in the boardroom than on a board, there's also a quality selection of clothing. **Map p. 43, 1D** 8

FOOD

Bay Cities 1517 Lincoln Blvd., Santa Monica, (310) 395-8279, www.baycitiesitaliandeli.com. Packed with Italian oils, vinegars, pastas, sauces and more, plus a selection of Middle Eastern, Israeli, Argentinian and French foods. In business since 1925, this deli has become a real institution—huge sandwich lines at lunch, but the hot, crusty loaves of bread come out of the oven all day long. **Map p. 42, 3C** 9

GIFTS

Daisy Arts 1312 Abbot Kinney Boulevard, (310) 396-8463, www.daisyarts.com. Owner Daisy Carlson was introduced to the art of bookbinding while filming a documentary on Umbrian craftspeople. She stayed, became an apprentice, and now sells journals bound in fine Italian leather, as well as a range of handcrafted leather wallets, frames, humidors and, best of all, travel cases full of secret compartments. **Map p. 43, 3-4D** 10

Elevator 55 N. Venice Blvd. [at Pacific], 310-306-7020. Elevator was originally supposed to be an art gallery, and co-owners Zen Nishimura and Kevin Kelly have an art flair in their selection of stock, which includes their own lines, elevator and zen bunni. The charming space still acts as a revolving gallery, with shows of photography and artwork, but it's really a boho-Venice lifestyle that's for sale here. True to the gallery spirit, Monday they're open by appointment only—it's regular hours the rest of the week. **Map p. 43, 4D** 11

shop!

Giant Robot 2015 Sawtelle Blvd., (310) 478-1819, www.giantrobot.com. Cult Asian-American pop-culture mag Giant Robot brings its quirky aesthetic to this Japanese-restaurant-filled stretch of Sawtelle. Stocked with tons of toys, comics, stationary, clothes and collectibles—some imported from Japan, others created by young designers. **Off map p. 45, 1D** 12

Hey Kookla 1025 Montana Ave., 310-899-9499, www.heykookla.com. Run by a mother-daughter team with an incredible eye for desirable home furnishings, accessories and beauty products. Complimentary refreshments are served in the back garden of this charming brown bungalow—lemonade, tea and sometimes, if you're lucky, cookies. **Map p. 42, 1C** 13

Obsolete 222 Main St., Santa Monica, 310-399-0024, www.obsoleteinc.com. Sometimes a store isn't just a place to purchase things. The proprietors of Obsolete have created an unbelievable assemblage of objects made obsolete by modern technology; all the detritus of centuries past, collected in a Venice storefront and presented in a way that allows you to appreciate their somewhat lonely beauty. **Map p. 43, 2D** 14

Scentiments 1331 Abbot Kinney Blvd., (310) 399-4110. Lush arrangements and perfect blooms at this flower shop, which also stocks an array of things that you would want to put on the coffee table, next to your bouquet—vases, bowls, incense holders. **Map p. 43, 3-4D** 10

Strange Invisible Perfumes 1209 Abbot Kinney Blvd., (310) 314-1505, www.strangeinvisibleperfumes.com. Half chemistry lab, half Bond-girl bordello, Alexandra Balahoutis' (step-daughter of producer Jerry Bruckheimer) perfumery takes its name from Shakespeare's *Anthony and Cleopatra*. Balahoutis will custom-blend a scent for you, or you can try one of her signature scents. **Map p. 43, 3D** 15

HOME

Eames Office 2665 Main St., Santa Monica, (310) 396-5991, www.eamesoffice.com. Run by Eames Demetrios, grandson of California modernism pioneers Charles and Ray Eames, the gallery has a rotating series of exhibitions of photos, works and artifacts that draw on the family archives. The store carries Eames furniture, books, films (*Powers of Ten*) and gifts (House of Cards). Website has information on arranging a self-guided tour of the Eames House exteriors. **Map p. 43, 1D** 16

Le Sanctuaire 2710 Main St., Santa Monica, (310) 581-8999, www.le-sanctuaire.com. Stocks hard-to-find kitchen items for gourmets who like to look good. Find French Laundry chef Thomas Kellerman's line of tableware for Limoges and a stack of pricey cookbooks that should be kept far from the stovetop. **Map p. 43, 1D** 7

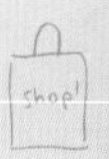

SHOES

Undefeated 2654 Main St., (310) 255-7995. A hit with sneaker heads from the day it opened, co-owner James Bond (yes, it's true!) stocks rare versions of big brands like Nike as well as boutique labels. Lots of events—art, music, shoe launches. **Map p. 43, 1D** 16

BEVERLY HILLS & WESTWOOD

There's not much shopping of note in Westwood, but if you're after high-end, big-label buys, a walk down Rodeo Dr. will take you past Chanel, Louis Vuitton, Hermes, Gucci, Prada and Armani, as well as some intrepid high street brands like BCBG and Lacoste.

BOOKS & GIFTS

Exoticar Model Gallery 9495 S. Santa Monica Blvd., Beverly Hills, (310) 276-5035, www.exoticar.com. Everything for the over-the-top auto enthusiast—die-cast car models and larger replicas, plus automotive art, hand-built models and even Diorama garage scenes. Car lover Jerry Seinfeld (he built an entire museum/garage for his beloved Porsches) shops here, as do Tim Allen and Jay Leno. **Map p. 44, 3C** 17

Taschen 354 N. Beverly Drive, Beverly Hills, (310) 274 4300, www.taschen.com. Computer-generated collages made of images from Taschen books past and present line the walls and ceiling, drawing you into lush, louche, slick, silly Taschen-world. Designed by Phillipe Starck, this is the German publisher's first US store; has hosted book parties for Rem Koolhaas, Hugh Hefner, Helmut Newton. **Map p. 44, 3D** 18

CLOTHES

Monique Lhuillier 9609 Santa Monica Blvd, Beverly Hills, (310) 550-3388 Poised to take Vera Wang's crown as the go-to bridal designer, Lhuillier did the wedding dress and bridesmaid gowns for Britney Spears' (second) surprise wedding. An ultra-feminine, beautifully detailed, modern-day princess look. **Map p. 44, 3C-D** 19

Prada 343 N. Rodeo Dr, Beverly Hills, (310) 278-8661, www.prada.com. This bastion of intelligent chic recently gave their Beverly Hills store a spectacular makeover by architect Rem Koolhaas, who insists that his Prada stores go beyond retail. Here he has created a virtual wonderland of design that nearly overshadows the clothes. **Map p. 44, 3D** 20

HOLLYWOOD & MIDTOWN

WEST HOLLYWOOD
MAK Center
A+D Museum
Runyon Canyon Park
Wattles Garden Park
Plummer Park
N La Brea Av
Sunset Blvd
Santa Monica Blvd
Hollywood Blvd
N Crescent Heights Blvd
Fountain Av
De Longpre Av
N Fairfax Av
N La Cienega Blvd
Holloway Dr
Laurel Canyon Blvd
Nichols Canyon Rd
Sunset Plaza Dr
Mount Olympus Dr
Rising Glen Rd
N San Vicente Blvd
N Doheny Dr
N Detroit St
N Formosa Av
N Alta Vista Blvd
N Poinsettia Pl
N Fuller Av
N Martel Av
N Vista St
N Gardner St
N Sierra Bonita Av
N Curson Av
N Stanley Av
N Spaulding Av
N Genesee Av
N Ogden Dr
N Orange Grove Av
N Hayworth Av
N Edinburgh Av
N Laurel Av
N Havenhurst Dr
N Kilkea Dr
N La Jolla Av
N Harper Av
N Sweetzer Av
N Flores St
N Kings Rd
N Orlando Av
N Croft Av
N Alfred St
Marmont Av
Hacienda Pl
Alta Loma Pl
West Knoll Dr
Westmount Dr
Westbourne Dr
Huntley Dr
Hancock Av
Palm Av
Larrabee St
Hilldale Av
Belfast Dr
Evanview Dr
Thrasher Av
Blue Jay Wy
Appian Wy
Lookout Mountain Av
Wonderland Av
Crescent Heights Blvd
Kirkwood Dr
Yucca Tr
Grandview Dr
Utica Dr
Gould Av
Electra Dr
Hercules Dr
Castair Dr
Wattles Dr
Outpost Dr
La Presa Dr
Cerrito Pl
Sycamore Av
Hillside Av
Franklin Av
Camino Palmero
Hawthorn Av
Selma Av
Courtney Av
Romaine St
Willoughby Av
Waring Av
Hampton Av
Lexington Av
Norton Av
Greenacre Av
Olive Dr
Queens Rd
Harold Wy
Kings Rd
Devlin Dr
Clark Dr
Wetherly Dr
Harratt St
Phyllis Av
Cynthia St
Vista Grande St
Dicks St
Norma Pl
Nellas St
Sherwood Dr
500 metres
A
B
C
D
1
2
3
4
86

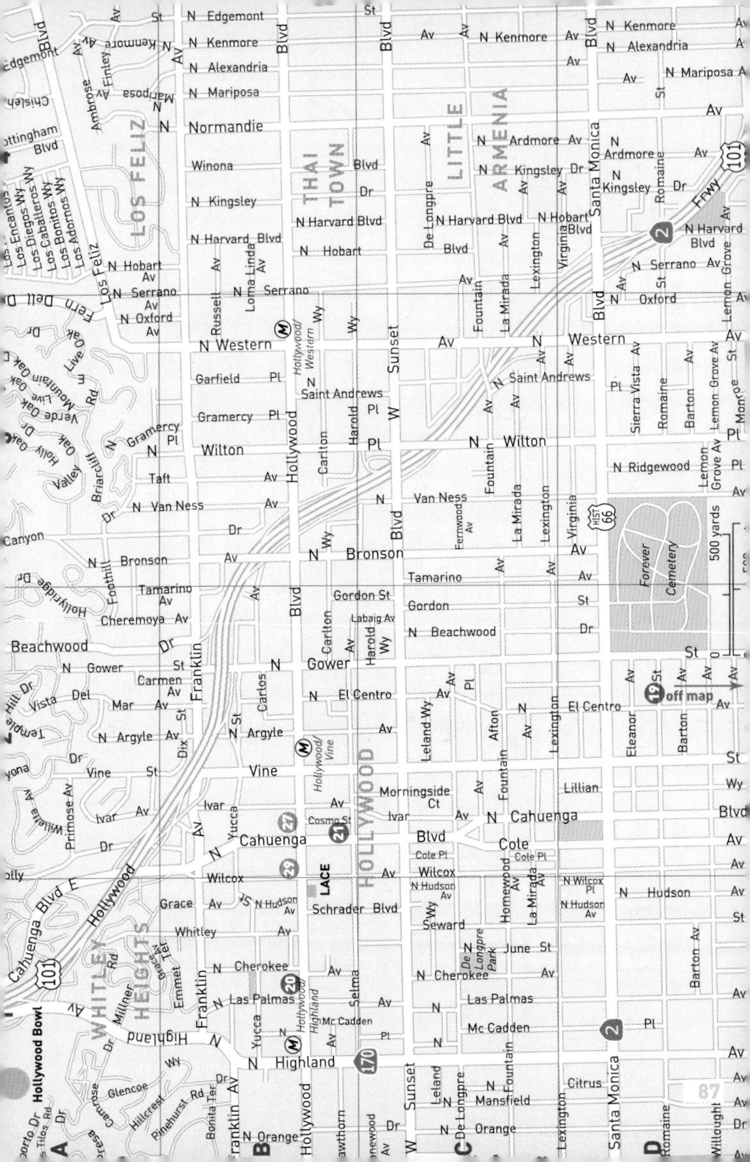

LOS FELIZ

THAI TOWN

LITTLE ARMENIA

HOLLYWOOD

WHITLEY HEIGHTS

Forever Cemetery

Hollywood Bowl

De Longpre Park

LACE

Hollywood/Western

Hollywood/Vine

Hollywood/Highland

off map

500 yards

A B C D

MIRACLE MILE

LA BREA PARK

SOUTH CARTHAY

Pan Pacific Park

Hancock Park

La Cienega Park

West Hollywood Park

Page Museum

La Brea Tar Pits

Craft and Folk Art Museum

LA County Museum of Art

Petersen Automotive Museum

Pacific Design Center

Kabbalah Centre

off map

500 yards

0

N La Brea Av
S La Brea Av
N Detroit St
S Detroit St
N Formosa Av
S Formosa Av
N Alta Vista Blvd
S Alta Vista Blvd
N Poinsettia Pl
S Poinsettia Pl
N Fuller Av
S Fuller Av
N Martel Av
S Martel Av
N Vista St
S Vista St
N Gardner St
S Gardner St
N Sierra Bonita Av
N Curson Av
N Stanley Av
N Spaulding Av
N Genesee Av
Genesee Av
N Ogden Dr
N Orange Grove Av
N Fairfax Av
S Fairfax Av
N Hayworth Av
N Edinburgh Av
N Laurel Av
N Crescent Heights Blvd
S Crescent Heights Blvd
N Kilkea Dr
N La Jolla Av
S La Jolla Av
N Harper Av
N Sweetzer Av
Sweetzer Av
N Flores St
N Kings Rd
N Orlando Av
Orlando Av
N Croft Av
N Alfred St
S Alfred St
N La Cienega Blvd
S La Cienega Blvd
Clinton St
Rosewood Av
Oakwood Av
Beverly Blvd
N Beverly Blvd
W 1st St
W 2nd St
W 3rd St
4th St
W 5th St
6th St
8th St
W 9th St
S Cloverdale Av
S Cochran Av
S Dunsmuir Av
S Burnside Av
Ridgeley Dr
Hauser Blvd
Masselin Av
S Sierra Bonita Av
S Curson Av
S Stanley Av
S Alandele Av
S Spaulding Av
S Genesee Av
S Ogden Dr
S Orange Grove Av
Gilmore Ln
Del Valle Dr
Barrows Dr
Commodore Sloat Dr
Hayes Dr
Moore Dr
Schumacher Dr
Tower Dr
N Gale Dr
S Gale Dr
N Hamilton Dr
S Hamilton Dr
Blackburn Av
Colgate Av
Drexel Av
Maryland Dr
Lindenhurst Av
S Orange Dr
Wilshire Blvd
San Vicente Blvd
S San Vicente Blvd
Olympic Blvd
Melrose Av
Westmount Dr
Westbourne Dr
Huntley Dr
Norwich Dr
N Sherbourne Dr
Bonner Dr
N Robertson Blvd
S Robertson Blvd
Rangely Av
Dorrington Av
Ashcroft Av
Almont Dr
N Le Doux Rd
S Le Doux Rd
N Stanley Dr
S Stanley Dr
Holt Av
N Carson Rd
S Carson Rd
S Sherbourne Dr
N Willaman Dr
S Willaman Dr
N Hamel Rd
S Hamel Dr
N Arnaz Dr
S Arnaz Dr
N Clark Dr
S Clark Dr
N Swall Dr
S Swall Dr
N La Peer Dr
S La Peer Dr
N Almont Dr
S Almont Dr
N Wetherly Dr
S Wetherly Dr
Alden Dr
Burton Wy
Dayton Wy
Clifton Wy
Charleville Blvd
Gregory Wy
Chalmers Dr
Corning St
Bedford St
Shenandoah St
Wooster St
Doheny Dr
N Doheny Dr
S Doheny Dr
S Oakhurst Dr
Harland Av
Nemo St
Santa Monica Blvd

1 2 3 4
A B C D

Halfway between downtown and the beach, the Midtown area is home to LACMA, the Pacific Design Center and scores of furniture shops. It is also the heart of three disparate communities: Orthodox Jews, Russian immigrants, and the gay and lesbian community of West Hollywood. It is not unusual to see two boys holding hands, on their way to a breakfast of organic *huevos rancheros*, crossing paths with a bearded man in a black overcoat and payes on his way to prayers. Aspiring actors and musicians fill the Spanish-style duplexes and four-plexes in the Fairfax area; for the few who make it big, the coveted next step is a mid-century-modern home in the surrounding Hollywood Hills. West Hollywood became an independent city in 1984; it's surely the only one in the world whose police squad cars sport a map of the city resembling an abstract version of the gay pride flag.

Hollywood is so famous you might think it doesn't need an introduction—but in fact this neighbourhood of LA is quite unlike what you've seen on the screen. Hollywood Blvd. was for many years seedy and run-down; recent attempts at gentrification, like the Kodak Theater with its epically proportioned elephant statues, seem to be working, if not quickly. Still, it is in Hollywood where much of LA's history lies, and the Midtown area is full of charming old homes along tree-lined streets and curious museums—about tar pits, cars or music, to name a few.

The Los Angeles County Museum of Art (LACMA)

OPEN	LACMA is open from 12 pm–8 pm, Mon, Tue and Thur; 12 pm–9 pm, Fri; 11 am–8 pm, Sat and Sun; closed Wednesday. LACMA West is open from 11 am–5 pm.
CHARGES	Regular admission $9; seniors over 62 $5; students with ID $5; children under 17 free. Free on the second Tuesday of each month and every day after 5 pm.
GUIDED VISITS	There are free, 50-minute docent-led tours of the permanent collection every afternoon—call or check website for exact times and topics. Shorter 'In Focus Talks' (20 minutes) on a particular artist or movement and 'Spotlight Talks' (15 minutes) on a particular work are given several times a week. To arrange tours for groups of 20 or more call (323) 857-6107.
DISABLED ACCESS	Fully wheelchair-accessible, elevator located immediately inside the Wilshire Blvd. entrance. Wheelchairs, assistive listening devices are available at the information centre.
SERVICES	Two museum stores, open during regular museum hours; reading room, café, restaurant
TELEPHONE	(323) 857-6000
WEB	www.lacma.org
MAIN ENTRANCE	5905 Wilshire Blvd.
GETTING THERE	By bus: 20, 21 or 720 By car: From the 10 freeway take the Fairfax Ave. exit north. Park in the museum's lot on Wilshire and Spaulding or Wilshire and Ogden.
EXTRAS	Frequent film screenings, art talks, lectures. In summer there is a Friday Night Jazz series. Recently the museum has been hosting surprise all-night parties, announced by e-mail a few days in advance.

Eating at the Museum Pentimento Restaurant at LACMA, 5905 Wilshire Blvd., T (323) 857-6000, www.patinagroup.com. Star chef Joachim Splichal's Patina empire has a virtual lock on every restaurant attached to a cultural institution in LA – MOCA, the Disney Concert Hall, the Norton Simon, they all serve up some form of Splichal's trademark California cuisine. Familiarity may breed contempt, but it's easily dispelled by a bite of the two-tone chocolate cake or a glance at the spread of sandwiches brought out as part of the afternoon tea. Menus change seasonally, but the Pentimento Cobb Salad is always a good bet.

LACMA

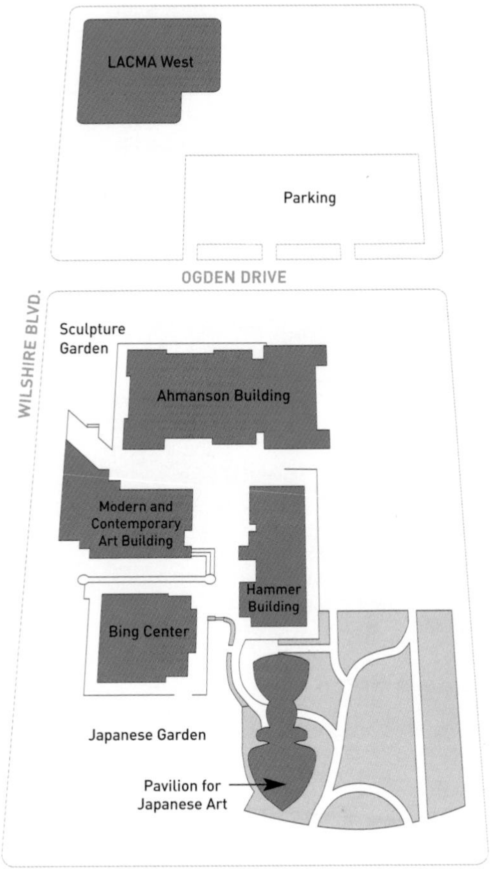

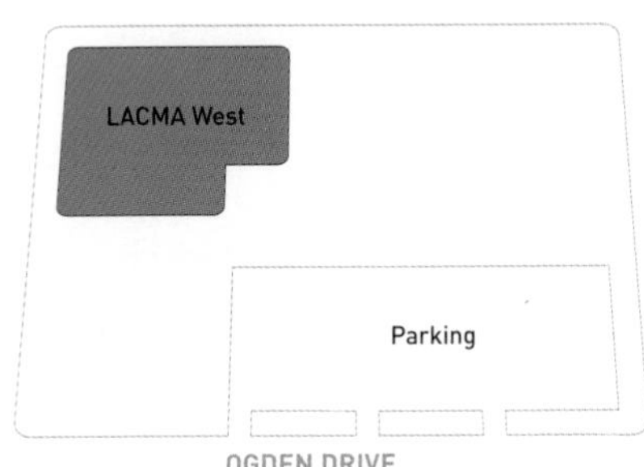

LACMA West
Parking
OGDEN DRIVE
WILSHIRE BLVD.
Sculpture Garden
Ahmanson Building
Modern and Contemporary Art Building
Hammer Building
Bing Center
Japanese Garden
Pavilion for Japanese Art

Millard Sheets *Angel's Flight* (1931)

HIGHLIGHTS

David Hockney's *Mulholland Drive*	Main collection
Jean Jacque Feuchere's *Satan*	
The netsuke collection	Japanese Pavilion
Margaret Kilgallen and Barry McGee's graffiti	Parking garage
Arbadil carpet	Islamic Art Collection

Sprawling, confusing and full of treasures, the Los Angeles County Museum of Art mirrors the city itself: it's housed in a group of buildings that range in style from mid-century modern to 1980s contempo-glitz, Art Deco to Googie-Japanese. The museum's extensive collections are just as wide-ranging. Outstanding examples of American painting, Japanese netsukes, Arts and Crafts furniture and Iranian textiles are all on permanent display; a recent special exhibition featured a stunning sand mandala created by Buddhist monks.

THE BUILDINGS

LACMA's three original buildings, designed by William Pereira, went up in 1965; today their solid yet graceful mid-century style is again in vogue. The 1980s kicked off a series of additions—very much of their time, with terra-cotta siding and the odd flash of neon—layered amongst the Pereira buildings around the museum's vaulted central plaza. Together the Ahmanson, Hammer and Modern & Contemporary Art Buildings and the Bing Center form the heart of the institution.

In 1988 LACMA added the Pavilion for Japanese Art. Picture a house for Fred Flintstone if he were a whimsical Japanese warrior-poet and you'll have a somewhat accurate image of this fantastic gallery (it's modelled on a Japanese *tokonoma*, an intimate alcove found in traditional teahouses). Architect Bruce Goff was an avid collector of Japanese woodblock prints; the hushed interior provides a perfect backdrop for their display. That same year the museum also built a winding sculpture garden off Wilshire Blvd.

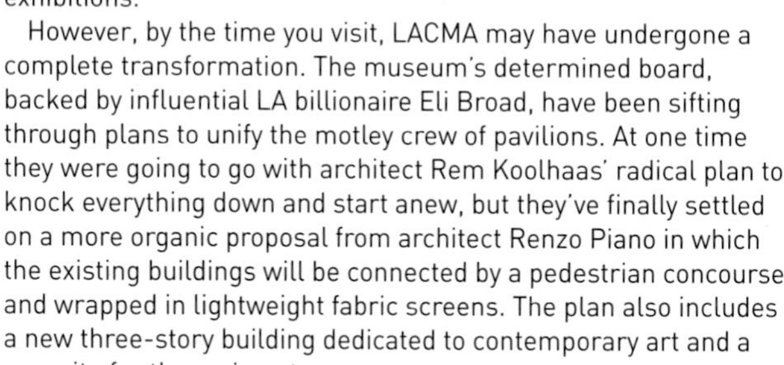

Less than a decade later, in 1994, the museum acquired the former May Company department store, an 1939 Art Deco building that now houses the Latin American art collection and LACMA Lab, an innovative children's gallery that is home to some of the museum's more experimental—and underappreciated—exhibitions.

However, by the time you visit, LACMA may have undergone a complete transformation. The museum's determined board, backed by influential LA billionaire Eli Broad, have been sifting through plans to unify the motley crew of pavilions. At one time they were going to go with architect Rem Koolhaas' radical plan to knock everything down and start anew, but they've finally settled on a more organic proposal from architect Renzo Piano in which the existing buildings will be connected by a pedestrian concourse and wrapped in lightweight fabric screens. The plan also includes a new three-story building dedicated to contemporary art and a new site for the main entrance.

There's a chance that the parking structure on Ogden St. will be razed, but before it is, be sure to stop by and search out the LACMA-commissioned graffiti by two amazing street artists, husband-and-wife team Margaret Kilgallen and Barry McGee. (This was the last piece that the two did together—Kilgallen died in 2001.)

THE COLLECTIONS

A complete catalogue of the more than 100,000 works in LACMA's possession would read like an Encyclopaedia Britannica of visual art, which is why the displays often change. When the museum was founded in 1910, it was part of the Museum of Science, History and Art at Exposition Park (see p. 18); the first painting that early institution acquired was **George Bellows**' *Cliff Dwellers* (1913), a straightforward and lively study of tenement life that prefigured the Ashcan School of painters. Cliff Dwellers set the tone for LACMA's renowned collection of *American Art*. Later additions include other instant classics of their time, like **Winslow Homer**'s sympathetic portrait of two female slaves, *The Cotton Pickers* (1876), and **Mary Cassatt**'s sweet but unsentimental *Mother About to Wash Her Sleepy Child* (1880). The American Art collection isn't all nobility and love—contemporary cartoonists like R. Crumb owe a debt to **Paul Cadmus**' *Coney Island* (1934), a satirical and lurid celebration of ugliness. Eighteenth-century painter **John Singleton Copley**, one of the first accomplished artists to be trained wholly in America, is well represented, as is the portrait master **John Singer Sargent** and early Impressionist **Childe Hassam**.

LACMA's *Decorative Arts* department is founded on a large donation from newspaper mogul William Randolph Hearst, whose love of the Renaissance is evident in his elaborate San Luis Obispo home, Hearst Castle, and also in the museum's repository of painted enamel from Limoges and medieval stained glass. The display of American decorative arts runs from the Rococo furniture of the 1750s–1780s, through the Federal Style, Greek and Roman-influenced neoclassicism and Renaissance revival (represented by a 14-foot rosewood pier mirror carved with Apollo and the muses, whose original mercury glass is still intact).

The *Arts and Crafts* collection is probably the finest in the country. With their reaction against the Industrial Age, designers like **Gustav Stickley** and **William Morris** had a profound influence on local and international style. Also, more recent furniture by mid-century Los Angeles-based designers like **Rudolph Schindler** and **Charles and Ray Eames** are also given the attention they deserve.

The majority of the museum's *Asian Art* collections are pre-19th-C. Chinese ceramics from the Shang dynasty to the Qing dynasty formed the core of the original collection, which has since expanded enormously—and comprehensively—to include Buddhist paintings from Korea's Choson period, a replica of a typical Chinese 'scholar's studio', Bronze Age objects from Indonesia's early Dongson culture, early Tibetan and Nepalese thanka paintings, a dagger once owned by the 17th-C Mughal emperor Aurangzeb and, most notably, a beautiful group of Chinese lacquers.

With so many questions and misconceptions about Islam floating around today, LACMA's superior collection of *Islamic Art* is an excellent entrée to the culture. The collection encompasses both religious art and art produced in countries under Islamic rule; works from the Syrian, Turkish and Byzantine empires are especially well-represented. The prophet Muhammad began to spread his teaching in the 7th C; as Islam took hold and the primacy of the Koran was established, calligraphy gained importance as an art form. LACMA has one particularly notable example of the Koran, written in Kufic script with gold ink on dyed blue parchment, that dates back to the 10th C. Chinese porcelains have been admired in the Muslim world for centuries, and beginning in the 9th C the Abbasid court produced pottery that emulated the pure white Chinese style of the time, glazing bowls in white but then adding geometric shapes in blues, greens and purples. The popularity of Chinese ceramics continued through to the late Islamic period of the 15th C. The Ottoman and Sufavid empires' artists emulated the style with ornate blue and white vases of their own design. Among the decorative art objects is the Ardabil carpet, one of the best-known Persian carpets in any collection. Part of a pair—the other hangs in the Victoria and Albert Museum in London—these intricate carpets were made in the 16th C for a shrine.

Because they're currently housed in LACMA West, two blocks away from the museum's main buildings, the *Latin American Art* collections are often overlooked. Particularly strong in modern Mexican masters, the bulk of the 2,500 pieces were acquired through a 1997 bequest from collectors Bernard and Edith Lewin. There are paintings and studies by muralists **Diego Rivera**, **Jose Clemento Orozco** and **David Alfaro Siqueiros**. **Jean Charlot**, a French-born muralist who in his twenties worked with Rivera and later was influential in developing and popularising mural art and Mexican themes, is given special attention. The influence of

European contemporaries like Matisse can be found in his emphasis on vibrant line and form, but the subjects that he found in Mexico give his work a very different sort of resonance.

LACMA's *Japanese Art* collection is also housed in a separate gallery, but this one's impossible to miss, on the east side of the museum compound, surrounded by a small Japanese garden. The works on paper—such as Edo period paintings, screens and scrolls—in this distinctive pavilion are arranged along an interior spiral walkway in dim alcoves that you can light to view, giving the entire exhibit a hushed, serene feel. Three additional galleries show ceramics and archaeological artefacts, prints from the Edo, Meiji, Taisho and Showa periods, and finely carved netsuke. The latter, especially, are not to be missed. Netsuke were walnut-sized toggles worn by men as part of a purse suspended from the kimono; the ordinary became art as the toggles evolved from simple wood or ivory pieces to carvings that depicted demons, maidens, scenes from famous plays or more unusual figures (LACMA's collection includes an 18th-C piece carved as a Dutchman in clogs). After the Meiji restoration of the mid-19th C, the Japanese largely switched to Western dress and netsuke were discarded or sold to European collectors, which means that the best collections—among which LACMA's belongs—are located outside Japan.

European Art is a valuable part of the museum's collections. The Italian Baroque paintings are renowned, but the museum's star—always on brochures and advertisement campaigns—is **Georges de la Tour**'s masterpiece, *Magdalen with the Smoking Flame* (1638-40). A bare-shouldered Mary Magdalen gazes at a flame; on her lap is a skull and in front of her are the Scriptures. Detail is simple but keenly observed, with the light and shadow of the candle creating a melancholy, contemplative world. Near the other end of the iconographic spectrum is **Jean-Jacque Feuchere**'s bronze sculpture of a bitter, brooding and very human-looking Satan, hunched over and engulfed by his own clawed wings (this Satan's pose reportedly inspired one of the world's best-known sculptures, Rodin's *Thinker*).

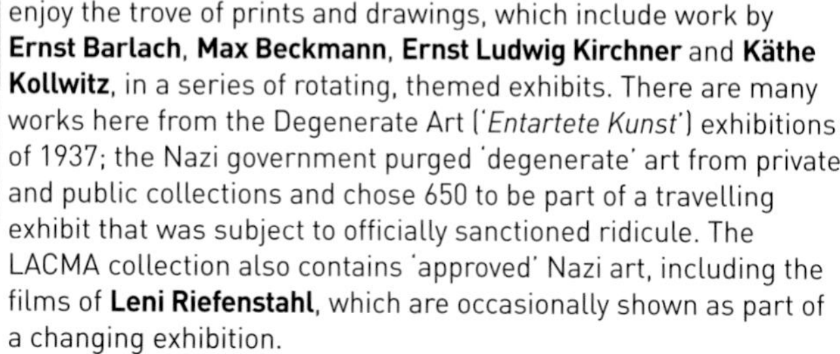

Los Angeles artists and German Expressionism are two of the most interesting components of LACMA's *Modern and Contemporary Art* collections. LACMA is home to the Rifkin Center of German Expressionist Studies, and though the study centre is only open to art historians and students, visitors are still able to enjoy the trove of prints and drawings, which include work by **Ernst Barlach**, **Max Beckmann**, **Ernst Ludwig Kirchner** and **Käthe Kollwitz**, in a series of rotating, themed exhibits. There are many works here from the Degenerate Art ('*Entartete Kunst*') exhibitions of 1937; the Nazi government purged 'degenerate' art from private and public collections and chose 650 to be part of a travelling exhibit that was subject to officially sanctioned ridicule. The LACMA collection also contains 'approved' Nazi art, including the films of **Leni Riefenstahl**, which are occasionally shown as part of a changing exhibition.

The *Modern European and American Art* galleries concentrate on work produced in Moscow, Paris and New York, with an especially comprehensive **Matisse** collection that includes several paintings and prints from his *Jazz* series.

Los Angeles-based artists like **Richard Diebenkorn** and **David Hockney** have pride of place in the *Contemporary Art* galleries, which focus on work after 1970. **Hockney**'s *Mulholland Drive, The Road to the Studio* (1980) is emblematic of his early work and demonstrates the strong influence of the city's mix of landscapes on local artists. Hockney came to Los Angeles in early 1964 and stayed, enamoured of the light and lifestyle. In many ways, his outsider's eye and affection for the landscape has made him LA's signature artist, despite the fact he is British.

in the area

A+D Museum 8560 W. Sunset Blvd., (310) 659-2445, www.aplusd.com. This free museum presents changing LA-related architecture and design exhibitions. The openings, which are open to the public, draw many of the city's top architects and design students. Also has a photography gallery with prints for purchase from photographers like Julius Shulman, who famously shot the Case Study houses. **Map p. 86, 2D**

Craft and Folk Art Museum 5814 Wilshire Blvd., (323) 937-4230, www.cafam.org. Combines folk art and contemporary arts and crafts to show things like hand-painted signs from Ghana, traditional Mexican silver, vintage Halloween costumes and hand-crafted kites. Helps host the popular Festival of Masks every autumn. **Map p. 88, 4D**

Hollyhock 817 Hilldale Ave., (310) 777-0100. Interior designer Suzanne Rheinstein's shop is worth a visit for a glimpse of Claes Oldenburg's giant Oldenburg Swiss Army Knife slicing through the roof. **Map p. 86, 1D**

Hollywood Bowl Museum 2301 N. Highland Ave., (323) 850-2058, www.hollywoodbowl.org. The Hollywood Bowl, an 18,000-seat

The Hollywood Bowl in 1932

A 1954 Plymouth Ghia from the Petersen Automotive Museum

amphitheatre that first opened in 1922, is part of Hollywood history. Every star of the music world performed there, and every star of the screen had a season ticket. The museum, tucked away on the grounds, presents a trove of local history as seen through the events at the Bowl. There is a permanent interactive exhibit that includes rare archival footage and an audio history of concerts, plus changing shows on subjects such as 'Hollywood Goes to the Bowl', featuring photos of stars like Claudette Colbert and Bette Davis. The newest exhibit shows letters written by concert-goers through the years. Free admission. **Map p. 87, 1A**

Kabbalah Centre 1054 S. Robertson Blvd., www.kabbalah.com. If you're curious about that red string bracelet that keeps showing up on red-carpet shots, take a trip to the Kabbalah Centre where Rabbi Yehuda Berg has transformed this ancient form of Jewish mysticism rooted in the study of the Zohar into a trendy spiritualism practiced by Madonna. **Map p. 88, 1D**

L.A.C.E. (Los Angeles Contemporary Exhibitions) 6522 Hollywood Blvd., (323) 957-1777, www.artleak.org. A long-running exhibition space and support organisation for emerging and under-represented artists. Recently moved into a cool new space in Hollywood, holds popular special events and openings. Barbara Kruger, Ed Ruscha, Skip Arnold, Mike Kelley are all on the advisory board. **Map p. 87, 1B**

MAK Center/Schindler House 835 N. Kings Rd., (323) 651-1510, www.makcenter.org. Rudolph Schindler's two-family home with roof-top sleeping porches and sliding doors was built as an experiment in living and established his philosophy of 'space architecture'. The house is open to visitors, free admission 4 pm-6 pm Fri and every Sept. 10 (Schindler's birthday). **Map p. 86, 2D**

MOCA at the Pacific Design Center 8687 Melrose Ave., (310) 289-5223, www.moca.org. An arm of the downtown museum (see p. 11), located on the grounds of the Pacific Design Center, a blue and green behemoth designed by Cesar Pelli that houses over 150 interior design showrooms. The MOCA building is on the San Vincente Blvd. side and focuses on architecture and design, with occasional spillover exhibits from the museum's larger shows. Admission is free. Eat at **Astra West** ((310) 652-3003), on the 3rd floor of the PDC. This is NY chef Charlie Palmer's first West Coast venture. Decor, as might be expected, is sleek, modern and gorgeous, with a dramatic bar and plush seating. It's only open for lunch. **Map p. 88, 1A**

Page Museum/La Brea Tar Pits 5801 Wilshire Blvd., (323) 934-PAGE, www.tarpits.org. SUVs and limos have taken over the territory once roamed by sabre-toothed tigers and giant wooly mammoths, but visitors to the fascinating La Brea Tar Pits can still see the sticky hole where some of them met their doom. Preserved in the natural deposit of black asphalt (which is still oozing up) is one of the largest and most diverse groupings of plant and animal fossils in the world. **Map p. 88, 3-4D**

Petersen Automotive Museum 6060 Wilshire Blvd., (323) 930-2277, www.petersen.org. Yes, Angelenos are serious about their cars. This surprisingly interesting museum takes a cultural approach, exploring the evolution of the car and its impact on our lives. The museum has over 300,000 feet of exhibits and life-size dioramas that feature race cars, classic cars, hot rods, motorcycles and cars from film. A special exhibit on at the moment presents wonderful examples of 'concept cars' from 1935 to 1955, a time when hope in technology drove creative innovation. **Map p. 88, 3C-D**

commercial galleries

THE 6150 WILSHIRE BLVD COMPLEX - Map p. 88, 3C ❶

Owned by art collector and former California State Senator Alan Serioty, in a former Lanz Clothiers building just blocks from LACMA, converted to house a group of seven galleries.

Acme Gallery (323) 857-5942, www.acmelosangeles.com. The anchor gallery in this complex exhibits well-known national and international artists, with especial loyalty to Uta Barth and Joyce Lightbody, two of the gallery's first artists.

Karyn Lovegrove Gallery (323) 525-1755, www.karynlovegrove gallery.com. Run by a young Australian transplant who brings in artists from her homeland, along with a keen selection of international talent.

Ace Gallery 5514 Wilshire Blvd., (323) 935-4411, www.acegallery.net. A huge space in one of the last LA buildings that has a doorman-operated lift. Work by established and emerging artists, both US and international. Strong on recent conceptual art. **Map p. 88, 4D** ❷

Fahey/Klein Gallery 148 N. La Brea Ave., (323) 934-2250, www.faheyklein gallery.com. Photography from high-profile artists like Irving Penn, Herb Ritts and Robert Graham. **Map p. 88, 4B** ❸

Jan Baum Gallery 170 S. La Brea Ave., (323) 932-0170, www.janbaum.com. African and East Asian masks and sculpture mix with contemporary art. **Map p. 88, 4B** ❹

Kantor Gallery 8642 Melrose Ave., (310) 659-5388, www.kantor gallery.com. This respected gallery shows both local artists heavily influenced by pop culture and an array of big-name artists like Keith Haring, Jean Michel Basquiat and Andy Warhol. **Map p. 88, 1A** ❺

Louis Stern Fine Arts 9002 Melrose Ave., (310) 276-014. www.louissternfinearts.com. One of the few LA galleries to deal in Impressionism, with work by Monet and Renoir, plus contemporary shows of established artists. **Map p. 88, 1A ❻**

Margo Leavin Gallery 812 N. Robertson Blvd., (310) 273-0604. Next door to the Hollyhock store, with its Claes Oldenburg knife (see p. 99), Margo Leavin has been showing contemporary painting, drawing and sculpture since 1970. Artists include John Baldesarri, Sol LeWitt, Louise Lawler. **Map p. 88, 1A ❼**

Newspace Gallery 5241 Melrose Ave., (323) 469-9353, www.newspacela.com. Another long-running local gallery, shows contemporary LA painting and sculpture and 20th-C masters including Roberts Rauschenberg, Dowd and Irwin. **Off map p. 88, 4A ❽**

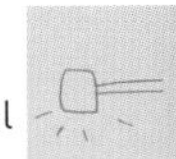

Stephen Cohen 7358 Beverly Blvd., (323) 937-5525, www.stephencohengallery.com. Cohen spearheads Photo L.A., an annual photo exhibition gathering over 80 galleries (visit website for more info). Shows photographers old (Weegee) and new (Lauren Greenfield). **Map p. 88, 4B ❾**

Subliminal Projects 3780 Wilshire Blvd., (213) 383-9299, www.subliminalprojects.com. Started by Shepard Fairey, the graffiti propagandist who created the Obey Giant phenomenon, this gallery promotes collaborations between artists in different disciplines. On the second floor of the Wiltern Theatre building (see p. 151). **Off map p. 88, 4D ❿**

Solway Jones 5377 Wilshire Blvd., (323) 937-7354. Emerging and established contemporary artists, with an emphasis on conceptual art, often shows video works. **Map p. 88, 4D ⓫**

ARCHITECTS IN LOS ANGELES: NEUTRA AND SCHINDLER

The careers of Neutra and Schindler followed almost parallel trajectories. Both were Austrian emigrants who came to Los Angeles in the 1920s at the behest of Frank Lloyd Wright, and both worked on Wright's buildings at Barnsdall Park. They were friends and partners, and although they eventually fell out, they both influenced the landscape of Los Angeles.

The two were friends from school in Vienna; Schindler recommended Neutra to Wright and helped Neutra come to LA. When he first arrived, Neutra stayed at Schindler's house in West Hollywood and they formed a partnership, the most notable result of which was a

League of Nations design competition entry later exhibited in Europe. The fact that Schindler's name was somehow left off the exhibition boards may be part of the reason for their eventual falling out. Or it may have been due to competition between the two for the patronage of progressive architecture devotees Philip and Lea Lovell.

Schindler's **Lovell Beach House** (1925) is a seminal work of modern architecture, although at its time it remained somewhat outside the main current of mid-century modern that was booming in Los Angeles. The house is elevated on five free-standing concrete frames, with staircases winding through the exposed structure. Schindler uses glass for composition more than transparency, as evidenced in the glass slots in his own house and the de-Stijl-like mullion arrangements in the Lovell Beach House. Neutra's **Lovell Health House** (1928) in the Hollywood Hills was the first steel residence in the US and one of the first International Style buildings in Los Angeles. In many of Neutra's early works, horizontal bands of windows with thin metal mullions wrap around the building, while in later works the entire wall is replaced by full-height sliding glass doors.

Schindler was perhaps more inventive in form, working with different structural systems and adapting to the terrain, while Neutra adhered to a purity of volume and orthogonals, but both built extensively in Los Angeles (Silver Lake and Echo Park (see p. 35) are the best places to find virtual colonies of their work). Fittingly, Schindler's style speaks more of Los Angeles while Neutra's work, working in the International Style with its ideals of the machine and mass production, was more easily reproduced elsewhere.

eat

RESTAURANTS

$ **Absolutely Phobulous** 350 N. La Cienega Blvd., (310) 360-3930. How can you pass up a restaurant with a name like this? Well-designed and inexpensive, this tiny spot serves up the popular Vietnamese soup known as *pho*. The rice noodles in the traditional beef broth (or the LA version, chicken broth) are topped with thinly sliced beef, chicken, seafood or vegetables, and accompanied by fresh basil and Vietnamese hot sauce. If you stop in for lunch, try the *banh mi* sandwich, a baguette filled with grilled meat, pickled and fresh vegetables. **Map p. 88, 2B** ❶

Boule Bakery 420 N. La Cienega Blvd., (310) 289-9977. No bread is baked at Boule, but pastry chef Michelle Myers, who co-owns Sona with her chef husband David Myers, does serve some delicious gourmet sandwiches. Most of the offerings at this sweet, robins-egg-blue patisserie tend towards gem-like delicacy, such as artisinal chocolates, perfect pastries and macaroons in high-brow flavours like lemon, rose and black truffle. **Map p. 88, 2A** ❷

Chao Krung 111 N. Fairfax Ave., (323) 932-9482, www.chaokrung.com. Waitresses dressed in shimmering updates of traditional Thai costumes welcome you into this dimly lit eatery decorated with carved teak panels and Burmese tapestries. Photojournalists who covered the Vietnamese war made this a regular meeting spot, and though they've faded away it's easy to imagine world-weary vets drinking beneath the sala roof that covers the bar. The food is exceptional—all the traditional Thai dishes, made with fresh, high-quality ingredients. The $10 lunch buffet is very popular. **Map p. 88, 3B** ❸

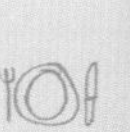

Joan's on 3rd 8350 W. 3rd St., (323) 655-1967, www.joansonthird.com. Lunchtime can be chaotic at this gourmet takeout spot, with a well-dressed West Hollywood crowd jockeying for the few sidewalk tables. Assemble a salad trio with choices like the tarragon chicken salad, or opt for a turkey meatloaf sandwich with chili aioli—either way, you should finish it off with a slice of their chocolate cake or one of the universally beloved cupcakes. Also a market full of foodie delights. **Map p. 88, 2B** ❹

Farmers Market, at 3rd and Fairfax Sceptics thought that the construction of the Grove shopping complex (see p. 114) would spell trouble for the historic Farmers Market, but it just brought in a whole new generation of strollers and snackers. Farmers Market started in 1934 as a simple collection of produce stands; it has become a vibrant gathering place for a real cross-section of the city. There are still farmers selling produce, but most people come here for the eclectic array of food stalls. The iconic

Mexican playing cards decorating the façade of **Loteria Grill** (Stall #322, (323) 930-2211, www.loteriagrill.com) make it easy to spot amidst the bustle of the market. The sublime *carne deshebrada*, dished onto a fresh corn tortilla and topped with soft Mexican cheese, is the choice for carnivores. If seafood is more your style, the best (and one of the only) oyster po'boys in the city can be found at **The Gumbo Pot** (Stall #312, (323) 933-0358, www.thegumbopotla.com), which also makes its signature gumbo, jambalaya and fresh beignets, dusted with powdered sugar. **Bob's Donuts** (Stall #450, (323) 933-8929) sells doughnuts to rival Krispy Kremes—and they've have been making bear claws and perfect glazed doughnuts for over thirty years. **Map p. 88, 3B** ❺

Mani's Bakery 519 S. Fairfax Avenue, (323) 938-8800, www.manis bakery.com. Don't be put off by the wheat-free, fat-free, vegan or low-carb signs—though it caters to some of the city's pickiest palates, Mani's manages to make its black bottom banana cream tarts creamy and its fruit-juice-sweetened Interrogation cupcake satisfyingly chocolate-y. The café food is less determinedly healthy, with a delicious turkey burger, thin and crispy fries and excellent soups served with a generous bread basket. Open late. **Map p. 88, 3C** ❻

Mickey & Sam's 8158 W. Sunset Blvd., (323) 656-8332. This under-appreciated café in a mini-mall across the street from the Sunset 5 Theatres is a mandatory stop for lovers of gelato. The owners—a young Korean couple who named the place after their sons—experiment with flavours like cream cheese or tomato, but also make smooth, creamy, not-too-sweet standbys, including an especially good chocolate hazelnut. Also a simple menu of sandwiches, salads and soup. **Map p. 86, 3B** 7

Versailles 1415 S. La Cienega Blvd., (323) 289-0392. A local chain that turns out countless platters of their signature dish—half a plump roast chicken, skin crisp and crackling, doused with heady garlic sauce and served with plantains, rice and black beans. There's a full menu of Cuban dishes, but if it's your first time, get a pitcher of sangria and the chicken (you can convince your dining companion to order something else to try: the oxtail stew, maybe, or the roast pork). **Off map**

Tail O'the Pup 329 N. San Vicente Blvd. [at Beverly], (310) 652-4517. Forget about the somewhat overrated and always overcrowded Pinks, wouldn't you rather eat your chilli cheese dog at a stand that is, in fact, shaped like a giant wiener (complete with bun)? Built in 1945, this 'mustard'-slathered stand is one of the last examples of LA's brief love affair with buildings that look like giant versions of what they sell or what they're named (like the now-demolished Brown Derby, a famous Hollywood restaurant shaped like, yes, a giant hat). Hamburgers and greasy breakfast specials are also available. **Map p. 88, 1-2A-B** 9

$$ **Angelini Osteria** 7313 Beverly Blvd., (323) 297-0070, www.angelini osteria.com. A cosy but minimalist storefront restaurant that has become a definite foodie destination. Italian country cooking at its Californian best, with dishes like lasagna verde with veal and beef ragout or whole branzino roasted in sea salt and aromatic herbs. Desserts are simple but pack a punch, especially the vanilla bean ice cream with a shot of espresso. **Map p. 88, 4B** 10

Hirozen 8385 Beverly Blvd., (323) 653-0470, www.hirozen.com. This tiny storefront is hidden in a completely non-descript mini-mall, but it's still almost always crowded with young agent and screenwriter types, talking up their next project over dishes of creative Japanese pub food and sushi that goes beyond the usual tuna and salmon. Chef Hiroji Obayashi has gone on to consult for hotels like the Bellagio, but still puts in time behind the counter. **Map p. 88, 2B** 11

$$$ **AOC** 8022 W. 3rd St., (323) 653-6359, www.aocwinebar.com. Caroline Styne and Suzanne Goin, formerly of Lucques, are responsible for reviving the wine bar in LA. You can choose half-glasses, glasses, carafes or full bottles from a fantastic list especially strong in French and California wines. The tapas-style dishes are small, but lend themselves to a tableful of tasting (request that they're not brought out all at once, as the tiny tables can't hold more than a few at a time). Chicken liver crostini, bacon-wrapped, parmesan-stuffed dates and frisee salad topped with a perfect fried egg are all good. **Map p. 88, 3B** ⓬

Campanile 624 S. La Brea Blvd., (323) 938-1447, www.campanilerestaurant.com. Architect Josh Schweitzer joined two 1929 buildings constructed for Charlie Chaplin's studios with a glass roof, and created a lovely, stone-walled atrium that houses Mark Peel and Nancy Silverton's California Mediterranean restaurant, consistently one of the best in the city. Come for the Monday Night Tasting menu, a three-course, $35 treat—a recent offering included steamed artichoke with aioli, oxtail stew with shell beans and baby carrots and a lemon sundae—or the Thursday Grilled Cheese Night. Next door is the La Brea Bakery. **Map p. 88, 4C** ⓭

Chameau 339 N. Fairfax Ave., (323) 951-0039. A hip Moroccan bistro with cool décor that mixes a spice market vibe with contemporary style—no belly dancers or overly ornate tapestries here. Instead, there are spicy lamb merguez sausages and a spectacular whole roasted loup de mer. **Map p. 88, 3A-B** ⓮

Sona 401 N. La Cienega Blvd., (310) 659-7708. Highbrow Asian fusion is the word of the day at chef David Myers' stark new spot. This restaurant is definitely a splurge, so its best to go all the way with one of the innovative tasting menus. Choose either the six-course or the nine-course and you'll be rewarded with a constantly changing series of small plates. Seafood dishes are always a triumph, and a strong Japanese influence shows in both the presentation and the simple contrast of textures. Desserts are delicious (the pastry chef just opened a bakery, Boule, across the street). **Map p. 88, 2A** ⓯

Table 8 7661 Melrose Ave., (323) 782-8258. Chef Govind Armstrong was discovered by Wolfgang Puck when he was just 11, so it's no surprise that he's a local restaurant star, cooking at Spago and Campanile. This luxe lounge offers up New American favourites like Porterhouse steak made with organic, farmers-market-fresh ingredients. The decor is surprisingly well-

Refreshment served old-style at Musso and Frank Grill

mannered, given its Melrose Ave. location below a tattoo parlour. Bar menu also available. **Map p. 88, 3A** ⑯

BARS

The Abbey 692 N. Robertson Blvd., (310) 289-8410, www.abbeyfoodandbar.com. A quick introduction to West Hollywood's boystown. Part coffee house, part lounge. The action goes on all day and far into the night. **Map p. 88, 1A** ⑰

El Carmen 8138 W. 3rd St., (323) 852-1552. A low-lit grotto hung with paintings of Mexican masked wrestlers. Tequila shots and margaritas are the drinks of choice here. **Map p. 88, 3B** ⑱

Forty Deuce 5574 Melrose Ave., (323) 466-6263, www.fortydeuce.com. This modern-day speakeasy always delivers a great time—sexy burlesque dancers who can really move, a live three-piece jazz band, and a very recognisable clientele. If you're ready for a big night, make a VIP reservation; it's $75, but includes drinks up to that amount and guarantees a table at this tiny club. **Off map p. 87, 2D** ⑲

Musso and Frank Grill 6667 Hollywood Blvd., (323) 467-7788. This quintessential old Hollywood watering hole, open since 1919, still makes some of the best martinis in town (see picture on previous page). Also a restaurant with a very old-fashioned menu (think iceberg lettuce salads). **Map p. 87, 1B** ⑳

Tokio 1640 Cahuenga Blvd., (323) 464-2065, www.tokiola.com. Co-owned by director Chris Weitz, Tokio's concept is Japanese-teahouse-meets-sexy-lounge, complete with saucy girls in geisha wear. Steps away from the still-popular Beauty Bar, both in the centre of Cahuenga's bar row, this is the stop for an evening of Japanese kitsch served Hollywood style. **Map p. 87, 2B** ㉑

LA STAIRWAYS

The hidden stairways of surprisingly hilly Los Angeles are like tiny ruptures in the urban fabric, steep and sudden. Discovering them is a wonderful way to see the city beyond the freeways.

The hillsides of Echo Park were built before cars became mass transport, and the more than two dozen public stairways act as sidewalks used by residents. The Echo Park Historical Society (call (323) 860-8874) offers walking tours of a few of these stairways, most notably the Baxter Stairs, which offer grand views from the top. Two other rewarding climbs in the area are the Laveta Terrace Stair and the Clinton Stair.

If you're looking for a public workout, the Santa Monica 4th Street Stairs (located at the north end of 4th St.) has health nuts, actors and investment bankers huffing and puffing past each other as they climb the tortuous canyon face. For a grander experience, the lavish and often-filmed Bunker Hill steps designed by Lawrence Halprin offer a fountain along its length, an escalator for the tired or out of shape, and a sculpture by Robert Graham in the plaza at the top.

shop

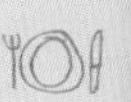

ACCESSORIES

Kaviar and Kind 8533 W. Sunset Blvd., (310) 659-8857. Designer Katherine Azarmi and co-owner Sunshine Ruffalo (wife of actor Mark Ruffalo) sell Azarmi's exquisite pieces, like a shimmering gold disc set with discreet diamonds and hung on a slim chain. Plus 30 other jewellery designers and a well-edited collection of accessories and furniture. Open by appointment only. **Map p. 86, 2C** 1

Kitson 115 S. Robertson Boulevard, (310) 859-2652, www.shopkitson.com. At Christmas, young Hollywood virtually sets up camp in this double storefront (steps away from the paparazzi-infested Ivy). Half the trends documented in gossip mags like *US Weekly* got their start in this sparkly shop: sequined tanks, Juicy Couture charm bracelets, Swarovski crystal studded pillboxes. Find it all here. **Map p. 88, 1B** 2

LA Eyeworks 7386 Beverly Blvd., (323) 931-7795, www.laeyeworks.com. Innovative window displays and a showroom designed by Neil Denari would make this an alluring shop even if they didn't have bold, stylish, statement-making frames. Founders Gai Gherrardi and Barbara McReynolds are art-world fixtures that never show up without their glasses. Great website. **Map p. 88, 4B** 3

shop

BOOKS

Bodhi Tree 8585 Melrose Blvd., (310) 659-1733, www.bodhitree.com. Anything that can be classified as 'spiritual' fits under the Bodhi Tree's branches, from astrology and tarot to metaphysical meditations and scholarly studies of Buddhism. It's the place to find a recommendation for a good reiki healer or a workshop on spirit guides. Once you've chosen a book, head over to the Urth Café or Elixir's tea garden. **Map p. 88, 2A** 4

Book Soup 8818 W. Sunset Blvd., (310) 659-3110, www.booksoup.com. In the heart of Sunset Strip, the floor-to-ceiling shelves of this literary lair are crowded with an excellent selection of art, film and design titles. An eclectic series of readings—recent guests have included Paris Hilton and Hunter S. Thompson. **Map p. 86, 1C-D** 5

Meltdown Comics 7522 W. Sunset Blvd., (323) 851-7283, www.meltcomics.com. More than just superhero stories. This superstore has an unbeatable collection of quirky, small press comics in the vein of Chris Ware and Adrian Tomine. Shows of local illustrators, and a selection of gifts and collectibles. Across the street is **Cheebo**, a cheerful spot for good gourmet slab pizzas and homemade potato chips. **Map p. 86, 4B** 6

Samuel French 7623 W. Sunset Blvd., (323) 876-0570, www.samuelfrench.com. The LA shop of a British script publisher (in operation since 1830), a hangout for local actors searching for monologues. Enormous selection of stage and screen plays, plus trade books, writing advice manuals and film history books. **Map p. 86, 3B** 7

Storyopolis 116 N. Robertson Blvd., (310) 358-2500, www.storyopolis.com. Every book you loved as a child is on the shelves here, along with contemporary volumes that are just as good. The art gallery exhibits children's book illustrators like Quentin Blake and Dr. Seuss, plus there are frequent arts and crafts events for kids and evening artists' studios for adults. **Map p. 88, 1B** 8

CLOTHES

Decades/Decades Two 8214 Melrose Ave., (323) 655-1960, www.decadestwo.com. When you see Nicole Kidman smirking on the red carpet in vintage Valentino, chances are she got it from retro-couturier Cameron Silver, the man almost single-handedly responsible for driving up the price of Pucci. Downstairs is Decades Two, which carries lower-priced, but equally fabulous, resale—think Chloe strawberry tops or Marni peasant shirts. **Map p. 88, 2A** 9

Eduardo Lucero 7378 Beverly Blvd., (323) 933-2778. Lucero's perfect tailoring and retro-glam look, inspired by his Latino heritage, made him a fast favourite of Madonna even when she was long out of her Evita phase. This atelier stocks red-carpet gowns for starlets and, sometimes, prom queens. **Map p. 88, 4B** 9

Fred Segal 8100 Melrose Ave. and in Santa Monica at 500 S. Broadway, (323) 651-4129. A boutique department store that is to Hollywood what the general store was to the American frontier. Every desirable denim brand is stocked here, plus upscale men's and women's clothing, shoes, accessories, gifts and an apothecary full of hard-to-find brands. Its location on Melrose west of Fairfax has been a magnet for like-minded stores—Emma Gold, Miu Miu, Xin, Agent Provocateur, Fornarina and Costume National are all within a couple of blocks. There's a large free parking lot. **Map p. 88, 3A** 10

The Grove 189 The Grove Dr., (888) 315-8883, www.thegrovela.com. Attached to the Farmers Market, this faux-Mediterranean village has transcended its Disney-like setting to become a favourite spot for shoppers. There are retail standbys like **Banana Republic**, **Abercrombie and Fitch** and the **Gap**, plus discount women's clothier **Forever 21** (an LA-based chain in constant trouble with sweatshop activists). **Anthropologie** offers boho-chic clothes and jewellery, the **Apple Shop** showcases Mac's latest (and offers free internet access), and a three-storey **Barnes and Noble** houses books, magazines and a Starbucks. **Map p. 88, 3B** 11

Jet Rag 825 N. La Brea Ave., (323) 939-0528. This trove of second-hand threads stands out for its selection, it neatness and its Sunday $1 car park sales. Very reasonably priced. **Map p. 86, 4D** 12

Maxfield Bleu 151 N. Robertson Blvd., (310) 275-7007. Discounted clothes from parent store Maxfield. When you're sorting through Gucci, Yojhi Yamamoto and Helmut Lang, even heavily marked-down items are still pricey, but there's a good selection and occasional sales. **Map p. 88, 1B** 13

Melrose Trading Post Corner of Fairfax and Melrose, (323) 655-7679. This Sunday flea market in the parking lot of Fairfax High School sells all the old furniture, costume jewellery and battered records that you'd expect, but there are also stalls set up by young designers and, every few weeks, discounted Jeffrey Campbell shoes. **Map p. 88, 3A** 14

Minkvox/Henry Duarte 8747 Sunset Blvd., (310) 652-5830. Rock and roll couturier Duarte makes custom-fitted jeans for musicians like Lenny

Kravitz, Sheryl Crow and Steven Tyler. Extraordinarily expensive, but each pair is hand-stitched with overlapping pieces that create equally extraordinary fit. **Map p. 86, 1C** 15

Naissance on Melrose 8350 Melrose Ave., (323) 653-8850, www.naissancematernity.com. For stylish mamas-to-be who still need to look good while they're fighting morning sickness. Some of the caftans and halter tops are so cute that even the non-baby-bearing will want to wear them. **Map p. 88, 2A** 16

South Willard 8038 W. 3rd St., (323) 653-6153. Under a striped awning, stylist Danielle Kays and boyfriend Ryan Conder stock avant-garde Belgian designers along with experimental LA locals. This is the place to find new fashion that's out of the usual California girl (silky tank top, snug jeans, cute heels) mould. **Map p. 88, 3B** 17

Suss Design 7350 Beverly Blvd., (323) 954-9637, www.sussdesign.com. Master knitter Suss Cousins helped make the grandmotherly art of needles and yarn hip with her multi-coloured ponchos and stylish sweaters. Ready-to-go kits for knit bikinis and pom pom hats are cute, if overpriced, but there's a great selection of yarns and occasional treasures in the bargain basket. A favourite among celebs, Suss also offers classes. **Map p. 88, 4B** 18

Trashy Lingerie 402 North La Cienega Blvd., (310) 652-4543, www.trashy.com. You'll have to buy a $5 'membership' to get in, but it's almost a rite of passage for the young ingénues that flood Hollywood. The thousands of designs include outrageous displays of lacy underthings and barely there Halloween costumes fit for the Playboy Mansion, all designed and made on the premises. **Map p. 88, 2A** 19

Turtle Beach Swimwear 320 S. La Cienega Blvd., (310) 652-6039, www.turtlebeachswim.com. It might not be anywhere near the beach, but the seamstresses here will be able to custom-fit you with a suit that will stay on when you're in the water and look good when you're lying on the sand. They have a library of fabrics and styles, plus racks of already-made suits. Prices for custom suits start at about $150. **Map p. 88, 2B** 20

Yellow 605 N. La Brea Blvd., (323) 525-0362. Owner Helen Hwang brings together American and European designers, cutting-edge and big-name, in her Asian-inspired two-storey boutique. There's play space for boys upstairs, with a DJ booth and video games, while downstairs glamour girls look through Dolce & Gabbana, Jill Stuart, Alice Roi, Sass & Bide. **Map p. 88, 4A** 21

GIFTS

Jonathan Adler 8125 Melrose Ave., (323) 658-8390, www.jonathanadler.com. With a style that's an endearing mix of mid-century Modern, subdued Hollywood Regency and Palm-Beach-by-way-of-Lily-Pulitzer, Jonathan Adler's shapely pots and lacquered boxes have attained a loyal following. Also furniture, textiles and now handbags. **Map p. 88, 3A** 22

Plastica 8405 W. 3rd St., (323) 655-1051, www.plasticashop.com. Life is fun at this tiny storefront full of bright toys and housewares, nearly all plastic. Look for glowing electric 'candles' shaped like little monsters, a deer's-head hanger, a rabbit radio and Rody, their signature inflatable horse. **Map p. 88, 2B** 23

OK 8303 W. 3rd St., (323) 653-3501. A narrow store with white walls and minimalist interior that make it feel almost like a design gallery. It sells beautiful hand-crafted glass vessels and an array of gifts and books. **Map p. 88, 2B** 24

Zipper 8316 W. 3rd St., (323) 951-0620, www.zippergifts.com. Like Kitson for adults, with goods more likely to show up on the pages of Vogue or In Style than US Weekly. Zipper fills its large space with an eclectic mix of items for home, office, kids and pets at every price range. **Map p. 88, 2B** 24

SHOES

Diavolina II 334 N. La Brea Blvd., (323) 936-5444, www.diavolinashoes.com. When you don't have to do too much walking, why not bedeck your feet in Veronique Branquinho, Olivier Theyskens or Alexander McQueen? Diavolina only stocks the sexy and the frivolous. **Map p. 88, 4A** 25

Sportie LA 7753 Melrose Ave., (323) 651-1553. Hip-hop heads and skaters have made a shrine of this over-stocked shop. Hard-to-find styles and colours from Nike, Puma, Adidas, Vans, Converse. **Map p. 88, 3A** 26

Star Shoes 6364 Hollywood Blvd., (323) 462-7827, www.starshoes.org. The confusing concept of this shoe store/bar used to be cocktails and vintage heels from Joseph LeRose, but now that kitten-heeled cobbler Hollywould has opened up a boutique in the bar, shoe buying has begun in earnest. **Map p. 87, 2B** 27

MISCELLANEOUS

Blackman/Cruz 800 N. La Cienega Blvd., (310) 657-9228, www.blackmancruz.com. Adam Blackman and David Cruz put their personal tastes to work assembling this collection of 19th- and 20th-C furniture, lighting and decorative arts. Many items are one-of-a-kind. **Map p. 86, 2D** 28

Cinema Collectors 1507 Wilcox Ave., (323) 461-6516. A dusty, crowded shop with a plethora of old posters and film stills. Search through black binders full of promo photos from movies past. **Map p. 87, 2B** 29

Samy's Camera 431 S. Fairfax Ave., (800) 321-4726, www.samys.com. An encyclopaedic selection of cameras, lenses, darkroom supplies, cases and photo books, with a knowledgeable staff that doesn't try too hard to sell. Also has vintage cameras and equipment. **Map p. 88, 3C** 30

Soolip Paperie & Press/Bungalow 8646 Melrose Ave., (310) 360-0545, www.soolip.com. From Japanese Yuzen silkscreens to embroidered paper from Jaipur, this paperie searches out unusual papers from around the world and presents them alongside handmade cards and leather-bound journals. For stylish Westsiders, Soolip has become the default choice for wedding invites and baby announcements. The Bungalow is a lifestyle store right behind the Paperie & Press. **Map p. 88, 1A** 31

The Wound and Wound Toy Co. 7374 Melrose Ave., (323) 653-6703, www.thewoundandwound.com. In the midst of Melrose's high street knock-off shops, this delightful toy store lines its walls with tin wind-up carousels, punching nun puppets, Astroboy figurines and vintage lunch boxes. **Map p. 88, 4A** 32

FILMING IN FILM CITY

Los Angeles has appeared on celluloid in so many guises, standing in for so many cities around the world, that it seems both distinctive and a blank slate, familiar without being notable. In many films, Los Angeles itself becomes part of the subject—the ocean becomes romance, suburbs or no-name motels stand in for alienation, the streets become a social scene.

The LA classic, on the top of anyone's list, is Roman Polanski's *Chinatown*. Mythologising the real-life figure of William Mulholland and the story of the LA aqueduct, Chinatown follows Jack Nicholson's P.I. Gittes as he travels throughout the city uncovering the backroom dealings that bring water to LA.

Other classics include Ripley Scott's sci-fi *Blade Runner*, with Harrison Ford as a bounty hunter in a post-apocalyptic LA (the Bradbury Building, mentioned on p. 18, features in the climax); the film adaptations of Raymond Chandler's novels, including *The Big Sleep* and *The Long Goodbye*; other noir films such as *Double Indemnity*; and Norma Desmond's star turn, ready for her close-up, in *Sunset Boulevard*. Neo-noir films include *The Grifters*, based on the book by Jim Thompson; also *Devil in a Blue Dress*, *The Limey*, and *L.A. Confidential* (with Neutra's Lovell House and the Crossroads of the World in leading roles).

The Southern California high school experience gave us valley girls and malls; while a genre by itself, these high school movies seem essentially Angeleno: Amy Heckerling's *Fast Times at Ridgemont High* and *Clueless*, George Lucas' *American Graffiti*, and in a different way, *Stand and Deliver*, based on the true story of a calculus teacher beating the odds in East LA.

For the older-but-not-quite-grown-up generation, there's Doug Liman's wannabe actors in *Swingers* and *Go*—the four-person, four-car driving parade is priceless. Antonioni's *Zabrieskie Point* follows two young lovers, idealistic and reckless, between Los Angeles and Death Valley. John Singleton's *Boyz N the Hood* has three childhood friends trying to escape the ghetto of South Central. Steve Martin's weatherman in *L.A. Story* finds love linked to weather—it's nice to find a movie that believes both can happen in the city. *Get Shorty*, based on a book by Elmore Leonard, gently skewers Hollywood.

Altman's *Short Cuts* is one of many ensemble pieces set in LA, with an earthquake linking separate lives. Quentin Tarentino's *Pulp Fiction* and *Jackie Brown* also move through many local spots.

Many directors take Los Angeles as a theme, exploring it in multiple films. Michael Mann's *Heat* and *Collateral* are driving tours of LA with gangster plots thrown in. Paul Thomas Anderson's *Boogie Nights* looks at the porn industry in the San Fernando Valley, *Magnolia* is an ensemble that sprawls over the city, and *Punch Drunk Love* turns the faceless warehouses bordering suburbia into a romantic setting. David Lynch's *Lost Highway* and *Mulholland Drive* offer beautiful and bizarre images of the city in the characteristic Lynch style.

There have been numerous sci-fi and disaster flicks filmed in LA: *Earthquake*, B-classic *Them!* where giant ants invade, *Terminator 2* and *Repo Man* with their car chases down the concrete channel of the LA River.

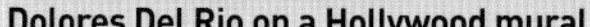

Dolores Del Rio on a Hollywood mural

The recent documentary by Thom Anderson, *Los Angeles Plays Itself*, is a compendium of the city's appearances on screen and serves as a useful guide for how it's been portrayed. Some of its discoveries include Kent Mackenzie's *The Exiles*, a semi-documentary about the indigenous community that lived on Bunker Hill before it was razed and redeveloped, and lesser-known films like Charles Burnett's *Killer of Sheep*, Haile Gerima's *Bush Mama* and Billy Woodberry's *Bless Their Little Hearts*. Another recent documentary, Stacy Peralta's *Dogtown and Z-Boys*, looks at the transformation of skater culture into an extreme sport.

PASADENA

The Millard House
The Gamble House
Fenyes Mansion
Norton Simon Museum
Armory Center for the Arts
Pasadena Memorial Park
Castle Green
Pasadena Central Park
Pasadena Museum of California Art
Pacific Asia Museum
Villaparke Center
Art Center College of Design
Garfield Park
PASADENA
SOUTH PASADENA
off map
Foothill
Colorado
Green
Del Mar
California
Fair Oaks
Los Robles
Lake
Orange Grove
Arroyo Pkwy
Long Beach Frwy
Walnut
Union
Holly
Memorial Park
Del Mar
Fillmore
Lake
500 m
500 yd

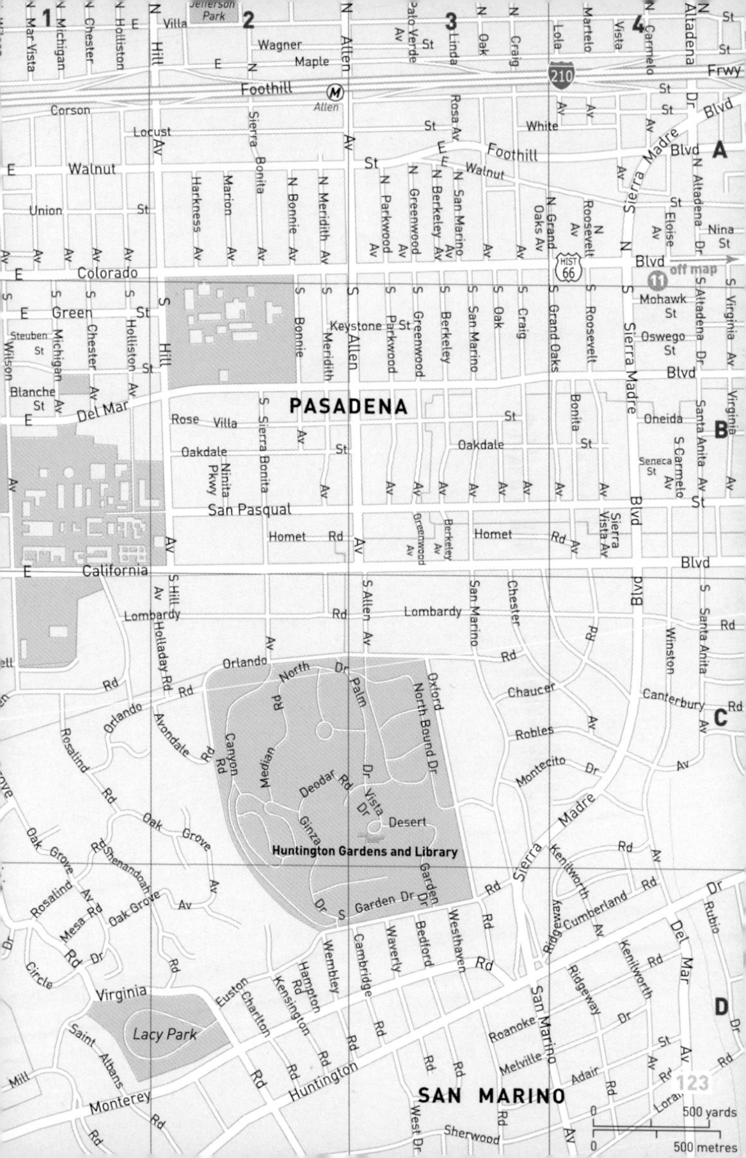
1
2
3
4
A
B
C
D
Jefferson Park
PASADENA
SAN MARINO
Huntington Gardens and Library
Lacy Park
Allen
210
HIST 66
11
off map
Frwy
Foothill
E Foothill Blvd
E Walnut St
E Colorado Blvd
E Green St
E Del Mar Blvd
E California Blvd
San Pasqual St
Corson
Locust
Union St
Villa
Wagner
Maple
White
Mohawk St
Oswego St
Steuben St
Blanche St
Rose Villa St
Oakdale St
Keystone St
Homet Rd
Lombardy Rd
Orlando Rd
Oneida
Seneca St
Nina St
Sierra Madre Blvd
Sierra Madre Villa Av
Huntington Dr
Monterey Rd
Virginia Rd
Chaucer
Robles Av
Montecito Dr
Canterbury Rd
Cumberland Rd
Roanoke
Melville
Adair
Sherwood
Lorain
N Mar Vista
N Michigan
N Chester
N Holliston
N Hill Av
N Allen Av
Palo Verde Av
N Linda Rosa Av
N Oak
N Craig
Lola Av
Martelo Av
Vista Av
N Carmelo Av
N Altadena Dr
Harkness Av
Marion Av
Sierra Bonita Av
N Bonnie Av
N Meridith Av
N Parkwood Av
N Greenwood Av
N Berkeley Av
N San Marino Av
Oaks Av
N Grand
N Roosevelt Av
Eloise Av
S Wilson
S Michigan
S Chester
S Holliston Av
S Hill Av
S Bonnie
S Meridith
S Allen Av
S Parkwood Av
S Greenwood Av
S Berkeley Av
S San Marino Av
S Oak Av
S Craig Av
S Grand Oaks Av
S Roosevelt
Bonita St
S Sierra Madre Blvd
S Altadena Dr
S Virginia Av
S Santa Anita Av
S Carmelo Av
Ninita Pkwy
S Sierra Bonita Av
Holladay Rd
Avondale Rd
Rosalind Rd
Oak Grove Av
Shenandoah Rd
Mesa Rd
Circle Dr
Saint Albans
Mill
Chester
Winston
Oxford
North Bound Dr
North Dr
Palm
Canyon Rd
Median Rd
Deodar Rd
Vista Dr
Ginza
Desert
Garden Dr
S Garden Dr
Euston
Charlton
Kensington Rd
Hampton Rd
Wembley
Cambridge Rd
Waverly Rd
Bedford Rd
Westhaven Rd
West Dr
Kenilworth Av
Ridgeway
San Marino Av
Del Mar Av
Rubio Dr
123
0 500 yards
0 500 metres

In 1771, Spanish priests found their way to the Pasadena area and erected California's fourth mission, the San Gabriel. The native Hahamogna tribe was enslaved and slowly died out, leaving the land in the hands of rancheros and church officials. By the 1920s, the orange groves gave way to stately homes and cultural attractions, and the city gained a reputation as a winter resort for upscale Easterners. It also had the west's first freeway, the Arroyo Seco ('Dry River') Parkway, built in 1940 and still in use today.

Pasadena still likes to cultivate that earlier, less cosmopolitan reputation; it gets as excited about the naming of the Rose Bowl princesses as it does about the California Institute of Technology's frequent Nobel Prizes. Though Angelenos may see this suburb as rather staid and old-money, as evidenced by the Norton Simon Museum and Huntington Library and Gardens, institutions like Art Center and Cal Tech have kept it growing, and for design-minded visitors, the abundance of Greene and Greene homes alone should make it worthwhile.

The Norton Simon Museum

OPEN	The Norton Simon is open 12 pm–6 pm, Tue–Thur, until 9 pm on Fri. Closed Monday.
CHARGES	Regular admission $6; seniors (62 and over) $3; students with ID or children under 18, free. Free admission on the first Friday of every month, 6 pm–9 pm.
GUIDED VISITS	Free themed tours on the first Friday of every month. Audio tours are $3, with an introduction by newscaster Tom Brokaw.
DISABLED ACCESS	Fully wheelchair accessible, wheelchairs available at the Coat Check. Guide dogs are allowed.
SERVICES	Gift shop, café, coat check. The Museum store and gardens close fifteen minutes before the galleries.
TELEPHONE	(626) 449-6840
WEB	www.nortonsimon.org
MAIN ENTRANCE	411 W. Colorado Blvd.
GETTING THERE	The free Pasadena ARTS Bus makes regular stops at the museum and throughout the city (visit www.ci.pasadena.ca.us for schedules). Metrolink: Gold Line to Memorial Park Station or bus 180/181. By car: 210 freeway west to the 134 east, Orange Grove exit. From the 110 north, Orange Grove exit. The large parking lot at the museum is free.
EXTRAS	Frequent hands-on family programmes and lectures by respected art historians. Two films are screened daily in the below-ground theatre: *The Art of Norton Simon*, narrated by Gregory Peck and made by Charles and Davis Guggenheim, and *Sister Wendy at the Norton Simon Museum*, with Sister Wendy Beckett.

HIGHLIGHTS

Degas' Ballerina sculptures	19th-C Gallery
Modigliani's *Portrait of the Artist's Wife*	20th-C Gallery
Rembrandt's *Self Portrait*	17th- and 18th-C European Art Gallery

THE NORTON SIMON MUSEUM

Theatre

Store

17th-
18th C

14th-
17th C

Sculpture Garden

20th C

19th C

MAIN LEVEL

South Asian

Special
Exhibitions

South Asian

LOWER LEVEL

Lucas Cranach's *Adam and Eve*	14th- to 17th-C
Raphael's *Madonna and Child with Book*	European Art Galleries
Guariento di Arpo's *Coronation of the Virgin* altarpiece	
Outdoor gardens, modelled after Monet's Giverny	
10th-C Shivalingam with Four Faces	South Asian Galleries

Norton Simon (1907–1993) was an entrepreneur who collected art as shrewdly and passionately as he collected businesses. With profits from a portfolio that included Hunt-Wesson Foods, McCall's Publishing, Canada Dry Corporation, Max Factor cosmetics, and Avis Car Rental, Simon amassed a selective but wide-ranging collection, especially strong on Dutch Old Masters like Rembrandt and Brueghel.

But in 1974, Norton Simon was a man with a stunning collection and no place to show it. The Pasadena Art Museum was a perpetually cash-strapped institution with a beautiful location in Carmelita Park and a reputation for producing critically praised but financially unsuccessful shows and exhibitions, mostly on contemporary art. The two joined forces and in October of 1975 reopened as the Norton Simon Museum of Art at Pasadena. The marriage was controversial, as Simon had little interest in contemporary art and jettisoned much of the Pasadena Art Museum's collection—including many works donated by artists—as soon as he could. Today, however, the Norton Simon is well-established as a museum with an excellent Impressionist and post-Impressionist collection, as well as a room that could serve as a primer on early 20th-C art. Simon married screen star Jennifer Jones in 1971; on a honeymoon to India, where the couple went in part because of Jones' devotion to yoga, he was inspired to collect Asian art, and began building his large concentration of Buddhist and Hindu statuary.

THE BUILDING

The museum building was begun in 1964 and completed in 1969 by the Pasadena-based architects Ladd & Kelsey. They filtered the influence of Pasadena's many Craftsman-style homes and arrived at an Asian-influenced Modernism that can be seen as a precursor to the Boho-Asian aesthetic that characterises so many of today's restaurants and residences. The building is lined in 115,000 umber tiles handmade by Edith Heath, a mid-century Modernist icon.

In the 1990s, the prolific Frank Gehry undertook a renovation of the museum's interiors, originally designed to show large pieces of modern art. Gehry reconfigured the galleries, replaced the dark parquet floors with French limestone, added a dramatic, sweeping spiral staircase and created skylights. He also worked on the Asian galleries, which are lined in red Indian sandstone and have views of the tranquil garden.

Inspired by Monet's garden at his home in Giverny, the Norton Simon's 79,000 square feet of garden are a perfect companion piece to the collection. Designed by landscape architect Nancy Goslee Power, the gardens even have a pond of water lilies.

THE COLLECTION

As you enter the atrium lobby you're greeted by the towering ***Buddha Shakyamuni***, a 9th-C sandstone sculpture from the mysterious Mon-Dvaravati kingdom, a centre of Indian Buddhism in Thailand from the 6th to the 10th C. Benevolent and calm, knowing and unknowable, he sets the tone for this accessible, rich collection. With its unobtrusive wall text, the Norton Simon is more about taking in the art rather than about taking in lots of information about the artists. In many of the rooms work is carefully grouped so that the pieces echo one another and we get a sense of the time and place in which they were created.

19TH-CENTURY GALLERY

In the first room of the 19th-C gallery, for example, **Edgar Degas'** ballerina sculptures are displayed on simple wooden pedestals

scattered throughout the space, surrounded by **Vincent Van Gogh**'s early peasant paintings and a selection of works by **Eduoard Manet** and **Paul Cezanne**. There are dancers on pointe, stretching and at rest, as well as *The Little Dancer, Aged Fourteen*, the only sculpture Degas ever exhibited while he was alive. Originally cast in wax at two-thirds scale and dressed in real clothes, the dancer was modelled on a young ballerina in a working-class troupe, a fact that created a sensation when the sculpture was first shown. The young lady at the Norton Simon is a bronze recasting made after Degas' death.

The museum's extensive collection of these dancers in bronze extends to the next room, where they're paired with the artist's intimately observed sketches of women bathing and arranging their hair.

Among the museum's collection of French Impressionists is **Claude Monet**'s *Mouth of the Seine at Honfleur*, the first painting he exhibited in Paris. It was shown at the Salon of 1865, where it was critically praised, but somewhat overshadowed by the furore over **Manet**'s controversial nude, *Olympia*. Another contemporary, the wealthy **Jean-Frederic Bazille**, who provided financial support for Monet and Renoir, painted the alluring *Woman in Moorish Costume* (1869). Painted the year before he died, at 29, in the Franco-Prussian War, Bazille's choice of subject reflects 19th-C Europe's romantic fascination with the Orient.

A tiny alcove off the main room gives the visitor a chance to pause and concentrate on six little paintings: two **Renoir** nudes, a **Bonnard** Paris street scene and three delicately wrought **Boudin** beach scenes. As one of the first advocates of 'plein-air' sketching, Boudin was a major influence on the younger Monet, and encouraged the attention to light and reflection that came to characterise the Impressionists.

20TH-CENTURY GALLERY

In the first two rooms of the 20th-Century galleries there is a quartet of heads worth noting. Two bold **Picasso** bronzes, *Head of a Jester* (1905) and *Head of a Woman* (1909), and **Modigliani**'s *Portrait of the Artist's Wife* (see next page), hang right next to a death mask

Amedeo Modigliani *The Artist's Wife (Jeanne Huberterne)* (1918)

of Modigliani cast by Jacques Lipchitz. The first Picasso hints at the artist's sense of the absurd but is relatively realistic; the second is an early example of his move into Cubism. Modigliani's classic portrait of Jeanne Hebuterne, to whom he was married for the three years before his death, is painted in his distinctive style, influenced by African masks and by his friend, Brancusi. It's a bit of a shock to see that unmistakable face in the artist's own death mask—with his elongated nose, chin and forehead, he looks like one of his own portraits.

The largest of the 20th-C rooms reads like a greatest hits collection. A couple of collected, enigmatic **Paul Klee** works (*Possibilities at Sea*, *Two Heads*, both 1932) hang near a prototypical **Diego Rivera** (*The Flower Vendor, or Girl with Lilies*, 1941) and a **Braque** study in delineated figures (*Artist and Model*, 1939). **Giacometti**'s *Tall Figure IV* (1960) stands sentry along with **Brancusi**'s golden *Bird in Space* (1931)—created for the Maharaja of Indore—over **Henry Moore**'s loving *Family Group #1* (1949-1949). **Barbara Hepworth**'s *Sea Forms* and several symphonic **Kandinsky** works (including *Open Green*, 1923) finish off what almost seems like an 'Introduction to Art History' lecture. The Klees and Kandinskys come from the collection of Emmy Galka Scheyer, an influential art dealer who was instrumental in bringing together the group known as the 'Blue Four', which also included Jawlensky and Feininger. Her collection, which includes her correspondence with the artists, makes up an important part of the Norton Simon's 20th-C collection.

17TH- AND 18TH-CENTURY EUROPEAN ART GALLERY

Easily overlooked in a room of Dutch figures, still lifes and landscapes in the 17th- and 18th-Century European Art gallery is **Louise Moillon**'s *Still Life with Cherries, Strawberries, Gooseberries* (1630), one of the few examples of her work in America. Moillon was regarded as one of the finest botanical painters of her time; this still life was done when she was only 20. On the opposite wall is **Jan Brueghel the Elder**'s *An Arrangement of Flowers* (1620). One of Brueghel's more restrained compositions, it demonstrates the difference between French and Dutch painting of the time.

Johannes Corneliszoon Verspronck is one of the lesser-known Dutch Old Masters, but his *Portrait of a Lady* (1641) is one of the most striking and life-like portraits in the gallery. The personality of the sitter, assumed to be Trijntgen Adamsdr, the wife of Haarlem painter Thomas Wyck, beams humanity and good humour across the ages, despite her enormous starched and pleated ruff.

Rembrandt, on the other hand, remains the most famous of the group. An obsessive self-portraitist, the museum has an excellent example in *Self Portrait* (1636–1638). He is wearing a beret, which was part of a typical artist's costume even then, and a heavy chain to symbolise success.

14TH- TO 17TH-CENTURY EUROPEAN ART GALLERIES

Stepping back to the 14th–17th-C European Art galleries, the collection turns towards religious imagery. One of the notable exceptions is a room of still lifes dominated by **Frans Snyders**' dynamic *Still Life with Fruits and Vegetables*. A cornucopia of artichokes, melons, radishes, scallions, celery, asparagus, peaches, apricots, figs and more, it could be a handbook for modern-day heirloom gardeners, and Snyders is credited with enlivening the still life, giving it artistic validity and popularity.

In one of **Raphael**'s peerless Madonnas, *Madonna and Child with Book* (1503), the two gaze at each other adoringly while holding a small book open to the Nones, recited in monasteries to commemorate Christ's crucifixion; Raphael plays to the intellect as well as the emotions. One of the most haunting portraits here of Christ is **Hans Memling**'s *Christ Giving His Blessing* (1478). The German-born Memling was one of the stars of the Bruges art scene, in great demand for his portraiture and his religious triptychs. This stark, finely-crafted painting has a glow typical of his work, enhanced by the barely perceptible halo.

For anyone who thinks that emotional detachment and a wry take on life are conditions of the 20th C, please turn to **Lucas Cranach the Elder**'s *Adam and Eve* (1530), in which a puzzled, innocent-looking Adam faces a curly-tressed, entirely seductive Eve, whose breasts are as perfectly round as the apple she holds in her hand. Painted in the Mannerist aesthetic of the 16th C, this almost secular version of the first couple feels so modern that it's not hard to imagine the painting discomfiting fundamentalists today.

A small, gleaming room of gilded Italian religious paintings rounds off the gallery. **Guariento di Arpo**'s multi-panelled *Coronation of the Virgin* altarpiece (1344) is unusual in its size and excellent repair; it's thought to be the best example in an American collection.

SOUTH ASIAN GALLERIES

Downstairs are the sumptuous South Asian galleries. Though the Norton Simon's collection of Asian sculpture from India and Southeast Asia isn't as celebrated as its European sculptures and paintings, the secret, cave-like feel of the galleries will give you a sense of discovery. There are some noted bronzes of the 10th to 12th C, including the *Shiva Nataraja*, cast in Tamil Nadu. The holes in the base of the bronze were likely used to insert poles so that worshippers could carry it during rituals.

Another 10th-C Hindu artifact is the *Shivalingam with Four Faces*, a sandstone carving from Uttar Pradesh in India. As the destroyer in the Hindu trinity—accompanied by Brahma the creator and Vishnu the preserver—Shiva is often represented in phallic form. The Sanskrit word 'linga' can be literally translated to mean 'gender'; here we see four faces of Shiva, each focused in one of the four directions, as well as a symbolic fifth head that is represented by the smooth dome of the lingam.

Saturn's rings, a Voyager 2 picture from JPL

in the area

Armory Center for the Arts 145 N. Raymond Ave., (626) 792-5101, www.armoryarts.org. A community arts centre located in the old National Guard Armory; frequent music and dance performances, several galleries of local artists. **Map p. 122, 2A**

Art Center College of Design Hill Campus: 1700 Lida St., (626) 396-2200; South Campus: 950 S. Raymond Ave., (626) 396-2919, www.artcenter.edu. The top auto design school in the country. A walk through the sleek, black Craig Ellwood-designed building on the Hill Campus will take you past aspiring designers working on futuristic vehicles. The new South Campus is in an enormous wind tunnel where Boeing used to test their aircraft. **Map p. 122, 2C**

Castle Green 99 S. Raymond Ave., (626) 793 0359, www.castlegreen.com. An early centre of Pasadena's social life, where members of the Valley Hunt Club planned the Tournament of Roses parade. Once part of the enormous Hotel Green, this seven-story Moorish, Spanish and Victorian-influenced annex was built in 1898 and is now a 50-unit apartment building that can be toured by appointment. **Map p. 122, 2B**

Descanso Gardens 1418 Descanso Dr., (818) 952-4391, www.descanso.org. Over 100 acres of beautifully laid-out gardens, including a section of California native plants. It's known for its 20 acres of camellias, celebrated yearly during the Camellia Festival. Call or check website for events and times. **Off map**

Fenyes Mansion 470 W. Walnut St. [at Orange Grove Blvd.], (626) 577-1660, www.pasadenahistory.org. In this 1905 Beaux Arts palace on Pasadena's former 'Millionaire's Row', owners Adalbert and Eva Fenyes (herself a painter) once hosted elaborate parties for the top society and artists of the day. The mansion later became the Finnish Consulate and is now the headquarters of the Pasadena Museum of History. There's still a gallery of Finnish folk art, as well as docent-led tours. **Map p. 122, 1A**

The Gamble House 4 Westmoreland Place [at Walnut St.], (626) 793-3334, www.gamblehouse.org. This is one of the best examples of renowned Pasadena-based architects Greene & Greene's Japanese-influenced Craftsman bungalows. Furniture custom-built for the house is displayed, along with furniture from neighbouring Greene & Greene bungalows. It now looks even better than ever after an exterior facelift completed in 2004. Open Thur–Sun. **Map p. 122, 1A**

Huntington Gardens and Library 1151 Oxford Rd., (626) 405-2100 (for tea house reservations call (626) 683-8131), www.huntington.org. A Neo-Classical manor with gorgeously manicured grounds, this 207-acre estate has three galleries of 18th- and 19th-C British art, including Gainsborough's *Blue Boy*. There is also a world-class, six-million volume library that boasts a Gutenberg Bible and the earliest known edition of the *Canterbury*

Tales. The grounds include a traditional Japanese garden and examples of desert and subtropical landscapes. In the rose garden is the Rose Garden Tea Room, with its popular high tea ($15) of fresh scones and a buffet of finger sandwiches, fruits, cheeses and desserts. Reserve far in advance. **Map p. 123, 3C**

Jet Propulsion Laboratory 4800 Oak Grove Drive, (818) 354-4321, www.jpl.nasa.gov. JPL—managed for NASA by the California Institute of Technology—sent the rovers to Mars and the Voyager to Jupiter. They designed NASA's Deep Space Network and scientists on the 177-acre campus man an asteroid-tracking system. There's a months-long waiting list for the free weekly tours, which take you through the spacecraft assembly facility and the space flight operations facility, but it's worth trying to get a space. If you do, don't forget to bring ID. **Off map**

Kidspace Children's Museum Brookside Park, 480 N. Arroyo Blvd. [at W. Holly St.], (626) 449-9144. Reopened in December 2004 after

Attributed to Chobunsai Eishi *Courtesan Reclining by a Circular Window* (late 19th C) At the Pacific Asia Museum

a big-budget revamp, the new Kidspace shines, with indoor and outdoor exhibits on insects, seismology, palaeontology and environmental education. There are also two three-storey climbing towers and a new building planned for early 2006 with robotics, construction, engineering and health exhibits, plus a music and art studio. Open every day. **Off map**

The Millard House 645 Prospect Crescent. The first of Frank Lloyd Wright's textile block houses. He later used the technique on the Freeman, Ennis and Storer houses, all located in Los Angeles. The Millard house is about two blocks away from the Gamble House (see p. 135). **Map p. 122, 1A**

Pacific Asia Museum 46 N. Los Robles Ave. [at E. Colorado Blvd.], (626) 449-2742, www.pacificasiamuseum.org. Closed Mon and Tue, free admission on the fourth Fri of every month. Housed in the elegant Grace Nicholson Building and wrapped around a lovely Chinese courtyard, the museum focuses on objects from Asia and the Pacific Islands. Their collection of Chinese ceramics is especially good, as are the Buddhist sculptures and Japanese paintings and wood-block prints. Informative web guide on 'understanding the art of Buddhism'. **Map p. 122. 3A**

Pasadena Museum of California Art 490 E. Union St. [at S. Los Robles], (626) 568-3665, www.pmcaonline.org. The museum was founded by long-time Pasadena residents Robert and Arlene Oltman, who also live on the top floor of the museum's new, three-storey structure. The focus is solely on California art and artists from 1850 to the present—they've staked out their territory with a California Design Biennial, which opens May 2005. Admission is free on the first Friday of every month. **Map p. 122, 3A**

eat

Pasadena has had urban planners excited since the renovation and revitalisation of their 'Old Town'. The historic business district of the town declined during the 1940s, nearly becoming a slum. There was talk in the 1970s of attempting to save it, but throughout Southern California the trend was for making the new, not preserving the old, and so Old Town was slated for demolition. Preservationists fought to save the derelict neighbourhood and, just in time, new financing was found to save Colorado Blvd. Now it's a popular and successful shopping street. Most of the brick buildings were erected between 1880–1900 and several still retain early signage.

$ **Euro Pane** 950 E. Colorado Blvd., (626) 577-1828. The master baker here got her start at LA favourite La Brea Bakery. Euro Pane is not the most comfortable place to sit and linger, but the flakiness of the chocolate croissants and the creamy tartness of their lemon bars makes it worth a visit. Also good are the sandwiches on fresh-baked breads (for a whole new world of tastes try the egg salad on their popular rosemary currant bread). **Map p. 122, 4A** ❶

Pie n' Burger 913 E. California Blvd. [at South Lake Ave.], (626) 795-1123. Yep, pie and burger is exactly what you want to get at this 40-year-old burger stand. Fresh buns come wrapped in wax paper and piled with hand-pressed patties, lettuce, onion, pickles and thousand-island dressing—exactly what a burger should be. The pies are baked by the same man who's been baking them since 1971, and drinks are hand-mixed with syrup and soda water. **Map p. 122, 4C** ❷

Saladang Song 383 S. Fair Oaks Ave., (626) 793-5200. There are Saladang Song devotees that rave about the food and engage in heated debate over which is better—the new Saladang Song or the original Saladang, right next door. In truth the food is no better or worse than any other moderately priced Thai, but the surroundings are sensational. A front courtyard screened in by laser-cut sheets of metal patterned after traditional Thai textiles is the perfect place for drinks on a hot summer night, helped along by appetisers from a menu full of Thai street food. **Map p. 122, 2B** ❸

Memorabilia at Soda Jerks

Soda Jerks 219 S. Fair Oaks Ave., (626) 583-8031. Full of vintage collectibles that might have belonged to the coolest kid on the block in the 1950s. Dive in here for dessert after a long day of shopping in Old Town. The food is fine, but the big, fat ice cream sundaes are the real draw. Made with Fosselman's ice cream—a local brand that's incredibly creamy and not too sweet—the malts and shakes are almost impossible to drink through a straw. Open late for this part of town, until 10 pm, Sun–Thur, and until 11 pm on Fri and Sat. **Map p. 122, 2B** 4

Tibet/Nepal House 36 E. Holly St., (626) 585-9955, www.tibetnepalhouse.com. Cheerful and tasty, decorated with Buddhist statuary and Tibetan crafts. They claim to be the only Tibetan and Nepali restaurant in Southern California. The lunch buffet is a good introduction, but at these prices you can choose several appetisers. Try the *momocha* (fried dumplings) and the *chi phalay* (lightly fried chicken patties). **Map p. 122, 2A** 5

$$$ **Bistro 45** 45 S. Mentor Ave., (626) 795-2478, www.bistro45.com. One of Pasadena's standout restaurants for the last decade. It sprawls over several rooms, so it sometimes feels like the waiters are running, but a glass of wine from the extensive list (praised by *Wine Spectator*) should keep you relaxed. There's a small plates menu, along with full-size New American main courses like sautéed Ahi with roast mushroom strudel and rack of lamb with parmesan flan. Don't miss the chocolate soup. **Map p. 122, 4B** 6

Madre's 897 Granite Drive [at S. Lake Ave.], (626) 744-0900. One of the few Pasadena restaurants that sometimes draws a Hollywood crowd. They come out of curiosity, because this is J. Lo's way to add restaurateur to her list of careers. Named in honour of her mother, and run by her father, Madre's food is based on recipes from the Lopez family's native Puerto Rico (*tostones*, *empanadas*) and Cuba (braised oxtail). Decorated by Shabby Chic queen Rachel Ashwell; the inviting interiors are English country house by way of old Havana. **Map p. 122, 4B** 7

The Raymond 1250 South Fair Oaks Ave., (626) 441 3136, www.theraymond.com. This cosy house was once a caretaker's cottage for the grand Raymond Hotel (after the hotel failed during the Great Depression, the owner moved to the cottage). The Raymond restaurant has been in operation since 1978; cuisine here is New American with menus that change weekly. The set lunch and four-course set dinner are good deals. **Map p. 122, 2D** 8

Xiomara 69 N. Raymond Ave, (626) 796-3919, www.xiomara restaurant.com. Chef-owner Xiomara Ardolina started off as a classic French chef, but in the early 1990s she began to incorporate the flavours of her native Cuba into the menu at Xiomara's, and soon created her own version of Nuevo Latino. There's a Cuban-Chinese influence too, in dishes like the Chino-Cubano Arroz Fritos. Wash it all down with a Mambo, made with rum and fresh cane juice. **Map p. 122, 2A** 9

BARS

El Cholo Café 958 S. Fair Oaks Ave. [at Arlington Dr.], (626) 441-4353. There's been an El Cholo in Los Angeles since 1923, and they are quite willing to claim that along the way they invented nachos and premium margaritas. Whether it's true or not, these are still the best things on the menu at this Mission-style restaurant, where a cross-section of Pasadena's residents gather for margaritas in the courtyard at happy hour. Around the corner from Art Center's South Campus. **Map p. 122, 2C** 10

Neon at Freddie's 35er Bar

E's Wine Bar 115 E. Colorado Blvd, (626) 793-6544, www.eswinebar.com. A stylish lounge with a stellar wine list. Try the 'flights', matched groupings of three to five different wines, served with a small platter of cheese and crackers. Also serves excellent bistro food. **Map p. 122, 2A-B** 11

Freddie's 35er Bar 12 E. Colorado Blvd., (626) 356-9315. This dive has hardly changed since it opened in 1962. Straight-up bar, with no frills and no respect for changing trends. The bartenders are surly, yet people keep coming back. **Map p. 122, 2A-B** 12

shop

Half a mile west of the Norton Simon, Colorado Blvd. leads you into Old Town Pasadena, a hugely successful downtown revitalisation project that is often cited as a model for other cities. In recent years the boutiques have been edged out by bigger retailers, but there are still some standbys like old-school pawnshop **Crown City Loan & Jewelry Co.** (65 E. Colorado Blvd.). Overseas visitors especially will be interested in trendy mini-department store **Urban Outfitters** (139 W. Colorado Blvd.).

Further west is the even newer **Paseo Colorado** (280 E. Colorado Blvd), an outdoor shopping plaza designed to blend in with Pasadena's refined Mission style. Chains also prevail here, but cosmetics super-store **Sephora**, designer **Betsy Johnson** and luxe apothecary **Lather** are all good for browsing.

ANTIQUES

Pasadena Antique Center & Annex 480 S. Fair Oaks Ave. (626) 449-7706, www.pasadenaantiquecenter.com. Over 130 antique dealers are gathered in this 33,000-square-foot warehouse. Most specialise, and you'll find everything from vintage textiles to black memorabilia. Popular with set decorators. **Map p. 122, 2B** 1

Rose Bowl Flea Market 1001 Rose Bowl Dr., (626) 560-7469, www.rgcshows.com/rosebowl.asp. At this market, with over 2,200 vendors of all kinds, shopping is serious business—the pros arrive at 5 am to snatch up the best pieces. Open on the 2nd Sun of each month, with a sliding time-scale of admissions ($20, 5 am–7am; $15, 7 am–8 am; $10, 8 am–9 am; $7, 9 am–3 pm). After 3 pm, vendors begin to tear down, but you can wander in for free until 4.30 pm. **Off map p. 122, 1A** 2

BEAUTY SUPPLY

Pure Beauty 28 E. Colorado Boulevard, (626) 564-9550, www.purebeauty.com. Part of a rapidly growing local chain, this stylish store and spa offers visitors speciality facials and brands like DDF, Dermalogica and Murad. Staff is very knowledgeable. **Map p. 122, 2B** 3

BOOKSTORES

Distant Lands 56 S. Raymond Ave., (800) 310-3220 or (626) 449-3220, www.distantlands.com. Feed your wanderlust at this well-stocked travel bookstore. It stocks gadgets to use on the road, along with travel guides, history books, essay collections from well-known travel writers and many, many maps. **Map p. 122, 2B** 4

Fuller Seminary and Bookstore 509 E. Walnut St., (626) 584-5350, www.fullerseminarybookstore.com. Attached to the largest multi-denominational seminary in the States. Sit down with a cappuccino and books like *Finding God in the Movies*. **Map p. 122, 3A** 5

Vroman's Bookstore 695 E. Colorado Blvd, (626) 449-5320, www.vromans.com. Every writer on a book tour seems to stop by this enormous store; recent readers have included Ray Bradbury, James Ellroy and Tom Wolfe. Independently owned for over a century, this two-storey spot also has a range of crafty gifts and a coffee shop. **Map p. 122, 4A** 6

CLOTHES

B. Luu 340 E. Colorado Blvd., (626) 792-4140. Cool vibe with hip designers like Frankie B. and Katayone Adeli. **Map p. 122, 3A** 7

Elisa B. 12 Douglas Alley, 626-792-4746. A perfect little fashion closet, with dresses from Diane Von Furstenberg and Nanette Lepore, California casual from Three Dots, Citizens of Humanity and C&C, plus local unknowns and a well-chosen selection of jewellery. **Map p. 122, 2B** 8

Neo 39 39 E. Colorado Blvd., (626) 683-1257 Cool casual kicks in this trendy shoe shop. The look is more about athletic and casual street shoes. **Map p. 122, 2B** 3

Therapy 316 E. Colorado Blvd., (626) 568-9905. Good buys on brands like Theory, Rebecca Taylor, Diane von Furstenberg and Margaret O'Leary. **Map p. 122, 3A** 7

Valsurf 169 West Colorado Blvd., (626) 796-0668, www.valsurf.com. A descendant of the legendary surf shack opened by a San Fernando Valley family that loved to ride the waves. They were the first to carry Quicksilver, Hobie and O'Neill. Now they also have Stussy, Zoo Six and others, plus surf, skate and snow equipment. **Map p. 122, 2B** 9

FOOD

Leonidas Chocolate Café 49 W. Colorado Blvd., (626) 577-7121. A new venture from the popular Belgian chocolatier, and the place for rich, rich hot chocolate and cocoa-powdered desserts. Pick up a box of their Manon Cafés and Noisette Masquées. **Map p. 122, 2B** 8

Three Dog Bakery 24 Smith Alley, (626) 440-0443, www.threedog.com. With a menu full of doggone punny humour and gleaming bakery cases of tasty treats for canines and humans, this is the place to go if your dog needs a cookie 'bone' and a nice dish of water. Of course, if you have a princess of a pooch, there are options like the Ruffles—truffle-shaped, but chocolate-free, doggy indulgences. Tucked in a plaza in the Old Town district. **Map p. 122, 2A-B** 10

MUSIC

Poo-Bah Record Shop 2636 E. Colorado Blvd., (626) 449-3359 www.poobah.com. Still retains a bit of 1970s flair but sells more indie, punk and experimental rock. Feels like a neighbourhood clubhouse. **Off map p. 123, 4A** 11

READING THE CITY

In Los Angeles, fiction and non-fiction closely resemble each other. Even a straightforward history cannot avoid mythology, and the most fanciful fiction set in LA is always rooted in the sunlight, the freeways, the earthquakes—all elements at once metaphorical and true.

Literary giants passed through Los Angeles; they came for Hollywood money, hating LA, loving LA, having to leave, unable

to live anywhere else. Bertolt Brecht, William Faulkner, Thomas Mann, Anais Nin, Dorothy Parker, Thomas Pynchon, William Saroyan, Upton Sinclair, John Steinbeck, Gore Vidal and Tennessee Williams are a few of those who lived here at some time or another; none of their writing escaped the influence of this evocative setting.

In **Joan Didion**'s *Play It As It Lays*, the heroine circles endlessly on the freeways as a sedative for everyday life. **Nathanael West**'s *The Day of the Locust* begins with a young man hoping to make it big in the movies and ends in a post-apocalyptic riot.

Raymond Chandler seems to forget there's a sun in LA; it's perpetual night for detective **Philip Marlowe** in *The Big Sleep, Farewell, My Lovely, The Long Goodbye* and others.

The opening chapter of **John Fante**'s *Ask the Dust* reads like a virtual map of downtown as a young writer wanders and hopes.

F. Scott Fitzgerald's unfinished (but undoubtedly heading for a tragic ending) *The Last Tycoon* chronicles the movie studio system that many writers set out to exploit and ended up being exploited by. **Thomas Pynchon**'s *The Crying of Lot 49* offers a mythical California with signs waiting to be read in the landscape.

Evelyn Waugh's *The Loved One* is a satirical story of a British expatriate who enters the funeral business in LA. **Aldous Huxley**'s *After Many a Summer Dies The Swan* ridicules the narcissistic rich as an old man with money but no power over death chooses a useless immortality over a natural ending. **Christopher Isherwood**'s *A Single Man* draws upon his own experiences teaching at Los Angeles State College.

In this city of storytellers, truth puts up a good fight—non-fiction books about Los Angeles are just as riveting as the fiction. The history of Los Angeles is indivisible from the history of the region's water supply: **William L. Kahrl**'s *Water and Power*

and **Marc Reisner**'s *Cadillac Desert* offer vivid accounts. **Joan Didion**'s *The White Album* is a book of essays that captures the time and place of 1960s Los Angeles. **D.J. Waldie**'s *Holy Land* is a poetic memoir of suburbia told by a man who doesn't drive, while **Anais Nin**'s *Diaries* chronicle her Sapphic double life in New York and Los Angeles.

Mike Davis' alarmist *City of Quartz* and *Ecology of Disaster* will make you wonder why you came here in the first place. **Esther McCoy** was modern architecture's unofficial historian, and her books include *Five California Architects*, *Case Study Houses* and numerous monographs. **Reyner Banham**'s *Los Angeles: An Architecture of Four Ecologies* is a classic for architecture and urban design fans.

Every so often, an LA writer feels left out by his or her New York contemporaries and puts together an anthology; recent publications include *Writing L.A.: A Literary Anthology* (Library of America), which collects essays on the city by M.F.K. Fisher, William Faulkner, Bertolt Brecht, Evelyn Waugh, Octavio Paz, Joan Didion, Norman Mailer, Walter Mosley, Mona Simpson and Charles Mingus, to name a few. *Another City: Writing from Los Angeles* (City Lights) is a mix of poetry, fiction and essays, and you might want to take a look at *L.A. Exiles: A Guide to Los Angeles Writing* (Marsilio) and *Absolute Disaster: Fiction from Los Angeles* (Audio Literature).

One of the best guides to the literature of Los Angeles is *Imagining Los Angeles: A City in Fiction* (University of Nevada Press), a thorough and outstanding overview of the most important writers and works. *The Misread City: New Literary Los Angeles* (Red Hen Press) takes a look at what's happening now, with a collection of author profiles, literary journalism and essays that praise the greats and celebrate the unknowns.

entertainment

ENTERTAINMENT INFORMATION

For up-to-date listings and recommendations, check the following:

Los Angeles Times www.calendarlive.com. (registration required). LA's main newspaper; there is a weekend entertainment section in the Thursday edition.

LA Weekly www.laweekly.com. This free alternative weekly is available at many cafés and coffeehouses.

Los Angeles Magazine www.lamag.com. A monthly overview of city happenings

LA Downtown News www.downtownnews.com. Exclusively Downtown events and news

Flavorpill www.flavorpill.net. A savvy selection of local events

VENUES

CLASSICAL MUSIC

Colburn School of Performing Arts 200 S. Grand Ave. [at W. 3rd St.], (213) 621-2200, www.colburnschool.edu. In addition to the courses at this prestigious school, there are a number of classical recitals, some with free admission. **Map p. 9, 2B**

Da Camera Society (213) 477-2929, www.dacamera.org. A 'moveable musical feast' of classical concerts in historic spots like the Doheny Mansion, the newly restored Roosevelt Hotel and Pasadena's 1916 replica of Versailles' garden pavilion, Le Petit Trianon.

Dorothy Chandler Pavilion 135 N. Grand Ave. [at W. 1st St.], (213) 480-3232. This 3,200-seat auditorium is home to the Los Angeles Opera and the Los Angeles Master Chorale. **Map p. 9, 2B**

Hollywood Bowl 2301 N. Highland Ave., (323) 850-2000, www.hollywoodbowl.org. The summer home of the LA Philharmonic since 1922, this outdoor amphitheatre's distinctive bandshell was first designed by Lloyd Wright (Frank's son) in 1928. In 1970 Frank Gehry gave it an acoustic update, and in 2004 architects Hodgetts+Fung completed a total redesign that retained the 1920s Streamline Moderne style of the original. A summer tradition for many Angelenos, who come with a picnic and a bottle of wine. Tickets range from $2 for 'nosebleed' bench seats (up so high they joke that you can feel the altitude) to over $50 for box seating—that is, if you can get one, as they're usually sold out long in advance. For more about the Bowl, see p. 99. **Map p. 87, 1A**

UCLA Royce Hall & Schoenberg Hall (310) 825-2101, www.uclalive.org. Built in 1929, Royce Hall was modelled after an 11th-C Italian church. It has a proud history of world-famous performers—from George Gershwin to Philip Glass, Ella Fitzgerald to Frank Zappa—and an extraordinarily eclectic programme. You never know what's on: a seminar with a Hollywood film star, a string quartet, a ballet, a symphony or some avant-garde banging on tin cans. Schoenberg Hall is a smaller hall also on the campus, in the music school. **Map p. 45, 4C**

USC Thornton School of Music University Park (213) 740-1672, www.usc.edu/music. Closely affiliated with the classical radio station KUSC, the Thornton School of Music is home to the USC Thornton Symphony Orchestra, Chamber Orchestra, Contemporary Music Ensemble, Early Music Ensemble and many others, from choral groups to jazz combos. Tickets are sometimes free for students and fairly cheap for everybody else, at $3–15 ($25 for premium seats). **Map p. 8, 2C**

Walt Disney Concert Hall 111 S. Grand Ave. [at 1st St.], (213) 480-3232. Excellent acoustics and an enormous organ make an enviable home for the LA Philharmonic. The Green Umbrella series features avant-garde music. Attached is the 250-seat REDCAT Theatre, operated by CalArts. For more about the hall, see p. 16. **Map p. 9, 2B**

JAZZ & BLUES

Babe & Ricky's Inn 4339 Leimert Blvd. [at W. 43rd Place], (323) 295-9112, www.bluesbar.com. This has been the best place for live blues for nearly

40 years. Along with the nourishing music comes wholesome soul food: fried catfish, Laura's chicken. Tickets $8–15, Monday Jam Night with Southern chicken dinner $5. **Off map**

Catalina Bar & Grill 6725 W. Sunset Blvd. [at N. Las Palmas Ave.], (323) 466 2210, www.catalinajazzclub.com. A smooth and elegant atmosphere of orange lanterns and soft spotlights surround the likes of David Sanborn and Marcus Miller. **Map p. 87, 1C**

Harvelle's 1432 4th St. [at Broadway and Santa Monica Blvd.], (310) 395-1676, www.harvelles.com. Singing the blues (and some rock, funk and pop) since 1931. Early arrival can sometimes mean free admission. **Map p. 42, 2D**

Jazz Bakery 3233 Helms Ave. [between Venice Blvd. and Washington Blvd.], (310) 271-9039, www.jazzbakery.org. Jam takes on a whole new meaning at this bakery as you munch your muffins to the sound of wailing trumpets and shuffling drums. $5 to play or listen. **Map p. 46, 1B**

ROCK & POP

Avalon 1735 Vine St. [at Hollywood Blvd.], (323) 462-8900, www.avalonhollywood.com. Great club nights Thur–Sat, with a mix of hip hop and house. **Map p. 87, 2B**

Henry Fonda Theatre 6126 Hollywood Blvd. [at Gower St.], (213) 365-6311, www.henryfondatheater.com. This 1926 theatre was one of Hollywood's first legitimate venues. These days you can catch Broadway shows or rock, pop and electronica acts. **Map p. 87, 2B**

House of Blues 8430 W. Sunset Blvd., [at Olive Dr.], (323) 848-5100, www.hob.com. Although it's called the House of Blues, blues is just about the only thing you won't hear. Books everyone from 50 Cent to KC and the Sunshine Band; famous gospel brunch on Sun. **Map p. 86, 2C**

Kibbitz Room 419 N. Fairfax Ave. [at Oakwood Ave.], (323) 651-2030. Attached to the famous 24-hour Canter's Deli, the Kibbitz Room hosts singer/songwriter nights. **Map p. 88, 3A**

Knitting Factory 7021 Hollywood Blvd. [at Sycamore Ave.], (323) 462-0204. If you were imagining a few old grannies clattering away on their needles, making tasteless and unusable jumpers for Christmas, you'd be wrong—this establishment produces no garments but showcases acts like DJ Shadow, PJ Harvey and Badly Drawn Boy. **Map p. 87, 1B**

Largo 432 N Fairfax Ave. [at Rosewood Ave.], (323) 852-1073, www.largo-

The Orpheum Theater

la.com. Anyone who knows about good music knows about Jon Brion—he's in residency at this small club, which draws music biz types and trendy locals, on Fri. **Map p. 88, 3A**

McCabe's Guitar Shop 3101 Pico Blvd. [at 31st St.], (310) 828-4497, www.mccabes.com. As the name suggests, it's an acoustic music store and repair shop. But round the back is a little room where the legends of the folk and alternative scene have played. It's not glamorous—it's not even comfortable—but it's an experience. Tickets a mere $3 and instrument browsing is fantastic. **Map p. 42, 4A**

The Orpheum 825 S. Broadway Ave. Once a historic vaudeville theatre on the Orpheum circuit, this grandiose entertainment lost its lustre when the era of vaudeville came to an end. It's reopened as a lease event venue, and is known for its working Wurlitzer organ, still played. Renovations like this are due to the sterling work of the LA Conservancy, which leads walks of Downtown theatres. **Map p. 9, 2C**

The Roxy 9009 W. Sunset Blvd. [at Hammond St.], (310) 278-9457, www.theroxyonsunset.com. Great sound system, a large dance floor and a bar brimming with beer. What more do you need? Great bands? They have those, too. **Map p. 86, 1C**

Spaceland 1717 Silver Lake Blvd. [at Effie Street], (213) 833-2843, www.clubspaceland.com. One of the few places you can smoke (cigarettes) with relative impunity. Small and always full of music lovers and frolickers. Witness all sorts of expertise on the turntables. **Map p. 36, 3C**

Temple Bar 1026 Wilshire Blvd. [at 11th Street], Santa Monica, (310) 393-6611. Features bands a little off the beaten path. Despite being located on one of Los Angeles' artery roads, this is a low-key joint, high on atmosphere. Expect soul, funk, Latin, hip hop and jazz. **Map p. 42, 2C**

The Troubadour 9081 Santa Monica Blvd. [at Doheny Dr.], (310) 276-6168, www.troubadour.com. This is one of Los Angeles' oldest clubs for rock. More recently, this was the venue that broke Gomez. **Map p. 44, 4B**

The Wiltern 3790 Wilshire Blvd. [at Western Ave.], (213) 380-5005. Built in 1931, the Wiltern is a big Art Deco venue that features big stars: when it re-opened to the world in 2002 it was to the sound of the Rolling Stones and Bob Dylan. All kinds play here, from contemporary bands to the Trans-Siberian Orchestra. **Off map**

WORLD MUSIC

Grand Performances at California Plaza www.grandperformances.org. Free summer evening shows of music, dance and performance from around the world. **Map p. 9, 2B**

Santa Monica Pier 200 Santa Monica Pier, (310) 458-8900, www.santamonicapier.org. Free summer performance series, also includes outdoor film screenings. **Map p. 42, 3D**

THEATRE

Actor's Gang 6209 Santa Monica Blvd. [at N. El Centro Ave.], (323) 962-3759, www.theactorsgang.com. Tim Robbins was one of the early members of this long-running theatre group, which still stages challenging work in its new playhouse. **Map p. 87, 2D**

Da Poety Lounge At Fairfax High School, 7850 Melrose Ave. [at N. Orange Grove Ave.], (323) 653-4085, www.dapoetrylounge.com. Raucous, high-spirited spoken word night every Tuesday. **Map p. 88, 3A**

Ford Amphitheatre 2580 E. Cahuenga Blvd., (323) 461-3673, www.fordamphitheater.org. Nestled in the Hollywood Hills, this 1241-seat outdoor amphitheatre presents music and theatre from May to September. The 87-seat indoor theatre presents new plays all year round. **Off map p. 87, 1A**

Geffen Playhouse 10886 Le Conte Ave. [at the Veterans Administration Medical Center], (310) 208-5454, www.geffenplayhouse.com. Serious theatre, five plays per season. Some famous names from TV might do a stint onstage. **Map p. 45, 3C**

Highways Performance Space and Gallery 1651 18th St. [at Olympic Blvd.], (310) 315-1459, www.highwaysperformance.org. Challenging shows, including works by solo dramatic artists, small theatre groups, dance companies and spoken-word artists. Expect the unusual and provocative. Two galleries promote emerging artists. **Map p. 42, 3B**

Mark Taper Forum 135 N. Grand Ave. [at 1st St.], (213) 628-2772, www.taperahmanson.com. Home to Center Theater Group. The big-name and highbrow plays come here from New York; also develops original work. **Map p. 9, 2B**

Matrix Theatre 7657 Melrose Ave. [at Stanley Ave.], (323) 852-1445. Respected local theatre shows the work of new and established playwrights. **Map p. 88, 3A**

Pantages 6233 Hollywood Blvd., (323) 468-1770, www.broadwayla.org. This former vaudeville theatre now shows popular musicals like *Les Miserables* and *Chicago*. **Map p. 87, 2B**

Pasadena Playhouse 39 S. El Molino Ave., (626) 356-7529, www.pasadenaplayhouse.org. The first American theatre to stage Shakespeare's entire playlist. Does six productions a season, often premieres new plays and musicals. **Map p. 122, 4B**

Will Geer Theatricum Botanicum 1419 N Topanga Canyon Blvd., (310) 455-3723, www.theatricum.com. Off the map. A very special venue in Topanga Canyon, it gives a rustic setting for performances of Shakespeare and other classics. **Off map**

COMEDY

Groundlings 7307 Melrose Ave. [at Poinsettia Place], (323) 934-4747, www.groundlings.com. This breeding ground for *Saturday Night Live* comedy stars has almost a cult following. It does both scripted and improv comedy; Sunday night shows especially popular. **Map p. 88, 4A**

Ice House 24 Mentor Ave. [at Colorado Blvd.], (626) 577-9133, www.icehousecomedy.com. Known for child-safe but still funny stand-up acts. **Map p. 122, 4B**

Improv 8162 Melrose Ave., (323) 651-2583, www.improv.com. A comedy chain, with big-name comics and those on their way up. **Map p. 88, 3A**

Laugh Factory 8001 Sunset Blvd. [at Laurel Canyon Blvd.], (323) 656-1336, www.laughfactory.com. A hangout for working comedians; Monday's Latino night is very popular. **Map p. 86, 3B**

CINEMAS

Hollywood, Tinseltown, the Dream Factory...Los Angeles is the land of film, so it's not surprising that it's also a city of cinemas. There's nothing more fun than catching a film in a movie palace restored to its former glory, and the eclecticism of Los Angeles architecture means that there's always something to see. In addition, with so many film-obsessed people around, programming at the smaller art theatres is extremely good.

Arclight 6360 W. Sunset Blvd. [at Vine St.], (323) 464-1478, www.arclightcinemas.com. Hollywood's beloved 1963 Cineramadome had a near miss with demolition but has been since renovated and renamed. Plays first-runs; restaurant. **Map p. 87, 2C**

Cecchi Gori Fine Arts 8556 Wilshire Blvd. [at Le Doux Rd.], (310) 652-1330. Art house films are shown in a beautifully restored Art Deco theatre. **Map p. 88, 2C**

Cinespia at Hollywood Forever 6000 Santa Monica Blvd., www.cinespia.org. Classic Hollywood films shown in a legendary Hollywood cemetery—the quintessential only-in-LA experience. Bring blankets, a picnic and lots of wine. **Map p. 87, 2D**

Egyptian Theatre 6712 Hollywood Blvd. [at Las Palmas Ave.], (323) 466-3456, www.egyptiantheatre.com. This recently restored 1922 gem (with fake pharaohs; the palm trees are real, though) is home to the American Cinematheque's excellent retrospective film series. It's next door to the historic Pig & Whistle restaurant, now a Hollywood lounge. **Map p. 87, 1B**

Grauman's Chinese Theatre 6925 Hollywood Blvd. [at Orange Dr.], (323) 464-6266, www.graumanschinese.com. This is where you'll find Trigger's hoof prints and Marilyn Monroe's tiny handprints in cement. Now shows first-run films. It was built by film impresario Sid Grauman, who also built the Egyptian, just down the street. **Map p. 87, 1B**

New Beverly Cinema 7165 Beverly Blvd. [at Detroit St.], (323) 938-4038, www.michaelwilliams.com/beverlycinema. A shabby theatre with smart programming, all cleverly-matched double-bills. **Map p. 88, 4B**

Nuart Theatre 11272 Santa Monica Blvd. [at Sawtelle Blvd.], (310) 478-6379. An art house cinema and home of the Rocky Horror Picture Show

(Saturday at midnight). It's next door to the film-geek paradise Cinefile, a rental shop that stocks hard-to find films (see p. 80). **Map p. 45, 1D**

Silent Movie Theater 611 N. Fairfax Ave. [at Clinton St.], (323) 655-2510, www.silentmovietheatre.com. Musical accompaniment by a live organist and theatre staff dressed in 1920s costumes are part of the draw at the only silent film house in the world. **Map p. 88, 3A**

RADIO STATIONS

If you left the iPod at home, chances are you'll be flipping through a lot of radio stations as you drive from LACMA to the Norton Simon. LA has its fair share of shock jocks like Tom Leykis, but it's also home to one of the nation's best National Public Radio (NPR) stations, KCRW, at 89.9 FM. NPR is a bit like the BBC (albeit much smaller), offering a mix of intelligent reporting, cultural shows and eclectic music programming.

If you want some music, one of LA's most popular frequencies is alternative rock station KROQ, at 106.7 FM. Its DJs have broken significant musical ground, introducing musicians like David Bowie and the Sex Pistols to America, but it's less adventurous since media conglomerate Infinity bought it.

FM

88.9 KXLU Eclectic music (experimental, electronica, blues, folk and more)

89.9 KCRW NPR (and their own influential music show, Morning Becomes Eclectic)

91.5 KUSC Classical

101.1 KRTH All oldies

102.7 KIIS Top 40 (home of radio host Rick Dees)

105.9 KPWR Hip-hop and R&B (home of outsized afternoon host Big Boy, whom you'll see on posters throughout the city)

106.7 KROQ Alternative rock

AM

98 KFWB 24-hour news channel

690 XTRA Sport coverage

790 KABC Talk radio (home of Larry Elder, Sean Hannity and Paul Harvey)

GUIDED TOURS

Wandering around the city on your own (with, of course, a good guidebook in hand!) is usually a better way to see the sights than from the back of a crowded tour bus. But for the days when you'd rather be led around—be it on foot, by horse or by silver Cadillac—these are some excellent and truly fun tours.

Architecture Tours LA (323) 464-7868, www.architecturetoursla.com. Architectural historian Laura Massino runs her tours by area, taking visitors through historic theatres and Frank Lloyd Wright homes in Hollywood, Art Deco shops and Craftsman homes in the Hancock Park/Miracle Mile area, Greene & Greene houses in Pasadena and a wealth of historical buildings in Downtown LA. Good wheels are a tour guide's necessity in LA, and Massino doesn't disappoint—transportation is her shiny 1962 black Cadillac.

Dearly Departed Tours (323) 466-3696, www.dearlydepartedtours.com. If you subscribe to the theory that scandal is a dish best served cold—very, very cold—let tour guide and nerdy necrophiliac Scott Michaels pack you in his tomb buggy and lead you to notorious celebrity murder and death sites. The two-and-a-half hour tour departs from Hollywood, Thur–Sun at 1 pm, reservations a must.

LA Conservancy Walking Tours (213) 623-2489, www.laconservancy.org. This not-for-profit is dedicated to the conservation and renovation of historical LA landmarks and neighbourhoods. It offers frequent walking tours led by entertaining, well-informed guides. Choices include 'Art Deco in Downtown's Historic Core' (every Saturday), 'Union Station' (every third Saturday), 'Historic Spring Street' (every fourth Saturday), 'Angeleno Heights', one of the city's early suburbs, (every first Saturday) and the gorgeous 'Broadway Theatres' (every Saturday).

Next Stage Tours (626) 577-7880, www.nextstagetours.com. Long-time tour guide Marlene Gordon puts together affordable, custom-designed tours with interesting themes: 'Famous Insomniacs' (early morning flower market, produce market, sunrise views), 'LA Has Its Ups and Downs' (an escalator and elevator tour), 'Faith in LA' (includes the Crystal Cathedral and Our Lady of Angels) are a sample.

Sunset Ranch Friday Night Dinner Ride 3400 Beachwood Dr., (323) 469-5450, www.sunsetranchhollywood.com. Take a slow-paced, 90-minute horseback ride through Griffith Park to Viva Fresh, where you'll stop for dinner and plenty of margaritas. Then it's a slightly tipsy ride back under the stars, all for $50 (not including dinner and drinks). Sunset Ranch is located underneath the Hollywood sign.

Take My Mother, Please (323) 737-2200, www.takemymother please.com. High-energy tour guide Anne Block specialises in custom tours; the former actress started off escorting the demanding visiting relatives of busy studio execs. Tell her what you're interested in seeing and she'll design a perfect day, which includes travelling the city in the backseat of her signature silver Cadillac.

TV Tapings www.tvtix.com. There are a few movie studios that still offer tours—you can see Warner Brothers and Universal if you sign up early enough—but the best semi-backstage experience may still be a TV show taping. Jay Leno fans can easily obtain Tonight Show tickets; long-running game shows like Jeopardy and even popular sitcoms are also available. The website also has information on being an extra in a crowd scene, another interesting way to get a behind-the-scenes look at the Hollywood experience.

SPORT

Los Angeles has a strange mix of professional sport: there are two basketball teams, one baseball team (there may be another, as the Anaheim Angels are lobbying to become 'the Los Angeles Angels of Anaheim'), no American football (gridiron) team, and a football (except LA calls it soccer) team whose popularity and share of news coverage varies yearly. To buy tickets contact Ticketmaster (www.ticketmaster.com) or team websites.

Real baseball old-timers might still think of them as the Brooklyn **Dodgers**, but the Angelenos have had Dodger blue running in their veins since 1958. A summer game at Dodger stadium (1000 Elysian Park Ave., www.dodgers.com) is a real taste of traditional Americana: beer, roasted peanuts, fly balls and pre-game sandwiches at Phillipe's (see p. 26) with the rest of the crowd. The season runs from March to September.

Non-LA residents love to hate basketball team the **Lakers** (www.lakers.com) almost as much as San Francisco loves to hate Los Angeles. Though they're not as dominant as they were, the Lakers still give good game. They play at the Staples Center (1111 S. Figueroa St.) from October to April, with playoffs in May and June. The **Clippers** (www.clippers.com) are LA's other NBA team—a sort of hard-working younger brother to the **Lakers**. LA also has its very own women's (WNBA) franchise, the **Sparks** (www.wnba.com/sparks).

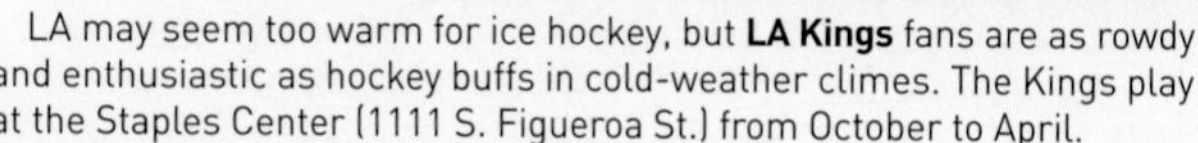

LA may seem too warm for ice hockey, but **LA Kings** fans are as rowdy and enthusiastic as hockey buffs in cold-weather climes. The Kings play at the Staples Center (1111 S. Figueroa St.) from October to April.

Football team **LA Galaxy** (www.lagalaxy.com) plays in the Home Depot Center (18400 Avalon Blvd.) from April to October, with play-offs in November. The Galaxy's stadium is also the training ground for the US National team.

ANNUAL FAIRS AND SHOWS

JANUARY

Jan 1 **The Tournament of Roses Parade** www.tournamentofroses.com. People start lining up along the parade route the night before, but you can still get a decent seat if you're willing to get up at the crack of dawn. The show starts at 8 am with elaborate floats covered entirely in organic materials—flowers and seeds, mostly—down Colorado Blvd. with baton twirlers, marching bands and horses in formation.

Second week **Greater LA Auto** Show www.laautoshow.com. All the manufacturing may be in Detroit, but Los Angeles is one of the centres of automotive design. The Auto Show is the place for designers to show off their futuristic prototypes. Held at the LA Convention Center.

FEBRUARY

All month **Whale watching** (310) 548-6279. This is when the gray whale migrates from Alaska to Baja, Mexico. Boats make trips out often, but you might need to book in advance.

Mid-February **Chinese New Year** Chinatown celebrates with floats and dancers on N. Broadway Blvd. near Spring St. **Map p. 9, 4A**

MARCH

First Sunday **City of Los Angeles Marathon** www.lamarathon.com This 26-mile course starts at Disney Hall and takes you through the city. A fun event.

Third week **The Academy Awards** Well, you probably aren't attending this one, but be wary if you're in Hollywood that night; streets will be blocked off for miles, causing jams and general frustration. Some people do line the roads, hoping for a glimpse of a famous face, but you're more likely to see only tinted windows. The awards are held at the Kodak Theatre on the corner of Hollywood Blvd. and Highland Ave. **Map p. 87, 1B**

Last weekend **The Blessing of the Animals** (see p. 38)

Easter **Easter Sunrise Service at the Hollywood Bowl** This multi-denominational ceremony, complete with choir and orchestra, has been going on for generations. It's beautiful to see the sun rise over the hills of Hollywood. (See p. 99 for more about the Hollywood Bowl).

MAY

May 5 **Cinco de Mayo** MacArthur Park (Off map p. 9) hosts one of the best festivals to celebrate the day. There's also one in in Pasadena at N. Garfield Ave. (Map p, 122, 3A). Ostensibly, Cinco de Mayo celebrates Mexico's defeat of the French army in a battle of 1862, but by now it's more about fun and laughter.

JUNE

Mid-month **Los Angeles Film Festival** www.lafilmfest.com See the most interesting films here in the film capital of the world. The festival shows around 70 features, 60 shorts, and 45 music videos each year; make sure to get tickets in advance.

Mid-month **Playboy Jazz Festival** The Hollywood Bowl (see p. 99) hosts this massive jazz festival. Bill Cosby is usually the MC; the line-up includes all the living greats.

AUGUST

First week **Surf Festival** www.surfestival.org. Lifeguards compete, as do civilians; the events are things like surfing, volleyball, swimming and sprinting through deep sand.

SEPTEMBER

Mid-month **Art in the Park** Staged by the Park La Brea Arts Council, www.parklabrea.com. Art, auctions and food, proceeds going to charity.

NOVEMBER

Last week **Hollywood Christmas Parade** The absolute best way to see B-level stars and this season's TV hotties, plus every year some better known celebrity acts as Grand Marshal. The marching bands and floats show that Hollywood still is just a little American town, for all its fame.

planning

WHEN TO GO

With blue skies nearly year-round, there is no bad time to be in LA, though sun worshippers may want to avoid the surprisingly overcast period of mid-to-late June. The best time of year to visit is April through early June, with highs starting in the low 20s (Celsius) and reaching the high 20s (70s to the mid-80s, Fahrenheit). The end of summer, from July to September, can be scorching, with temperatures that frequently reach the high 30s (up to 100° F); nights mercifully cool down to around 20°C (68°F). That's also the season of the hot, desert-born Santa Ana winds, a strange and restless time that Joan Didion called, 'the season of suicide and divorce and prickly dread, wherever the wind blows,' and when, said Raymond Chandler,'every booze party ends in a fight.'

Contrary to popular opinion, it does get cold in LA—temperatures start to drop in October, with highs around 20°C (the upper 60s F) and lows under 10°C (in the high 40s), though a mid-20s (80°F) Christmas is not unheard of. Rain—sometimes torrential—falls briefly in spring and autumn.

PASSPORTS & FORMALITIES

Most citizens of Visa Wavier Program countries do not need a visa, but do need to present a valid passport. Other foreign citizens will require a non-immigrant visa. A visa is also required if your stay is over 90 days or if you have a criminal conviction, medical ineligibility, have been denied entry or deported from the United States or overstayed on a previous visit. Getting a visa usually requires an interview and can take a few weeks, and with recently tightened security measures, it's best to plan well in advance. Bear in mind that you will need a machine-readable passport to enter the United States.

GETTING THERE

AIRPORTS

Most international and many domestic flights arrive at Los Angeles International Airport (LAX), the third-busiest airport in the world. LAX is close to the ocean, about 20 miles southwest of downtown Los Angeles. International flights also land at Ontario International Airport, located about 40 miles east in the Inland Empire. Other domestic airports include Long Beach Airport, about 25 miles south of downtown, John Wayne Airport, about 40 miles southeast in Orange County, and Burbank Airport, about 15 miles northwest in the San Fernando Valley. Budget airline Jet Blue flies out of Long Beach.

Los Angeles International Airport (LAX) (310) 646-5252

Ontario International Airport (ONT) (909) 937-2700

Long Beach Airport (562) 570-2619

John Wayne Airport (SNA) (949) 252-5200

Burbank Airport (BUR) (818) 840-8840

AIRLINES

American Airways (800) 433-7300, www.aa.com

Delta Airlines (800) 241-4141, www.delta.com

JetBlue Airways (800) 538-2583, www.jetblue.com

Northwest Airlines (800) 225-2525, www.nwa.com

Southwest Airlines (800) 435-9792, www.southwest.com

United Airlines (800) 241-6522, www.united.com

Virgin Airlines (800) 862-8621, www.fly.virgin.com

TRAVEL SITES

Cheap Tickets www.cheaptickets.com

Expedia www.expedia.com

Orbitz www.orbitz.com

Priceline www.priceline.com

Travelocity www.travelocity.com

TRAIN & BUS

Union Station (800 N. Alameda St. at Cesar Chavez Ave., (800) USA-RAIL, www.amtrak.com) serves commuter lines throughout Southern California as well as long-distance Amtrak trains.

Greyhound (800) 229-9424, www.greyhound.com. Greyhound is the major long-distance coach service within the US.

BY CAR

With its car culture, Los Angeles is at the centre of a network of freeways and highways that converge downtown. From the north and south, the most direct route is the I-5. The US-101 is more scenic and takes longer. The most beautiful, but slowest, route is the Pacific Coast Highway (PCH or Hwy 1), with its continuous view of the ocean. From the east, the I-10 travels in a straight line to Downtown and continues to the beach.

GETTING TO THE CITY

FROM THE AIRPORTS

PUBLIC TRANSPORT

There are Ground Transportation counters at all major airports, and Los Angeles World Airports operates a website (www.lawa.org) with a detailed section about ground transport.

The Metropolitan Transit Authority provides public transportation—via city bus and train—from LAX. A free shuttle takes passengers to the Metro Rail Green Line Aviation Station and to the Bus Center: (800) 266-6883, www.mta.net.

TAXIS

Taxis can be found kerbside at all airports. Only authorized taxis with an official seal from the LA Department of Transportation are allowed to operate in the airport. There is a $38 flat fare per trip (group) either direction, between LAX and Downtown and a $2.50 surcharge for all trips originating at LAX.

Authorized Taxicab Supervision (323) 776-5324

Beverly Hills Cab Company (310) 273-6611

Independent Taxi Owners Association (213) 666-0045

LA Taxi/United Checker Cab (213) 627-7000

LIMO SERVICES

Quick Limousine Service (877) 698-5555, www.quicklimousine service.com

LA Limo Rental (818) 761-5466, www.lalimorental.com

CAR RENTAL

Rental cars are available at all airports and are convenient for getting around the city during your stay. Many airlines and hotels offer discounts on car rental services.

Alamo (310) 649-2242; www.alamo.com

Dollar Rent-A-Car (213) 487-0303; www.dollar.com

Hertz (213) 625-1034; www.hertz.com

SHUTTLES

'Shared ride' vans provide shuttle services to all Southern California counties and are a cheap way to get to and from the airport.

Prime Time Shuttle (800) 733-8267, www.primetimeshuttle.com

SuperShuttle (310) 782-6600, www.supershuttle.com

GETTING AROUND

BY CAR

Los Angeles is a driver's city, and in fact is fairly easy to navigate. Still, there are a few things that can confuse visitors. Freeway signs can be misleading because they vary between identifying freeways by name and by number. Freeways can also be named for their terminus (the San Diego freeway) or the area they traverse (the 101 is the Hollywood freeway and also the Ventura freeway, depending on where you are). Southern Californians, almost without exception, refer to freeways as 'the something'—as in, 'Take the 10 to the 110, then get on the 5 North and take it to the 2'—a fact that confounds the grammatically conscientious visitor.

FREEWAYS BY NAME AND NUMBER

For a map of the freeways, turn to the back of the book.

2 – Glendale Freeway

5 – Santa Ana Freeway/Golden State Freeway

10 – Santa Monica Freeway/San Bernardino Freeway
60 – Pomona Freeway
90 – Marina Freeway
91 – Artesia Freeway/Riverside Freeway
101 – Ventura Freeway/Hollywood Freeway
110 – Pasadena Freeway/Harbor Freeway
118 – Simi Valley Freeway/San Fernando Valley Freeway
210 – Foothill Freeway
405 – San Diego Freeway
605 – San Gabriel Freeway
710 – Long Beach Freeway

BY PUBLIC TRANSPORT

Buses and subways are run by the Metropolitan Transit Authority. Maps are posted in subway stations and on buses, or call (800) COMMUTE. A handy Metro Trip Planner and information on schedules and routes can be found online at www.mta.net.

TRAVEL PASSES AND TICKETS

Basic bus and subway fare is $1.25. If you will be riding the bus or subway regularly during your visit, prepaid passes and tokens offer a good discount and are available at Metro Customer Centers and supermarkets, including Ralph's, Jon's Market, and Pavilions. A day pass is $3, weekly pass $14, two-week pass $27 and monthly pass $52. Day passes may be purchased on board any Metro bus or from a Metro Rail ticket vending machine. Two children under age 5 may travel free with each fare-paying adult on bus or rail. And remember, if you're paying the fare in cash, you must have exact change.

THE SUBWAY

See subway map on p. 192.

Yes, there is a subway system in Los Angeles. Granted, the route is short, but it links areas of interest and the art in the subways, sponsored by the Metro Art programme, is worth a trip in itself. Free two-hour tours are offered the first Saturday and Sunday of every month, call (213) 922-2738.

The Metro Rail system is comprised of the Blue, Green, Red and Gold Lines. The Blue Line runs north and south between Long Beach and Los Angeles. The Green Line crosses the Blue Line, running east and west between Norwalk and Redondo Beach, curving south near the Los Angeles International Airport. The Red Line subway meets the Blue Line in Los Angeles and provides service through Downtown, between Union Station, the Mid-Wilshire area, Hollywood and the San Fernando Valley. The Gold Line connects with the Red Line at Union Station, and runs northeast to Pasadena. Rail service runs from approximately 5 am until 12.30 am.

THE BUS

Buses are a bit slower-paced, but are a good way to see the city. Bike racks are attached to the front of the bus and passengers are responsible for securing and retrieving their bikes. Metro Rapid buses (they're a distinctive red) offer faster service at no extra charge; serving heavily travelled areas, they are more frequent, make fewer stops, and have special sensors to turn traffic lights green.

BY TAXIS

Taxis can be convenient if you're not going far, but the fare can be quite expensive if you're travelling from one side of town to the other. Don't expect to flag down a passing cab at any street corner; they can generally be found outside hotels, theatres, and some subway stations. Fares start at $2 with $0.20 for each additional 1/10 mile and $0.20 each 32 seconds of waiting or traffic delay time (a real possibility).

Call the City of Los Angeles Taxi Services if you have a complaint or question; for fares, areas served, and a list of taxi services, visit www.taxicabsla.org.

A few local cab companies:

Independent Taxi Company (800) 521-8294

LA Taxi (310) 715-1968

United Independent Taxi Drivers (323) 462-1088

Yellow Cab Company (888) 793-5569

SAFE TRAVELLING AFTER A FEW

Forget about the shiny white stretch limo or the 40-foot Hummer limo—a much saner option for a night out anywhere on the Westside is to drive your own car, then when you've had a few drinks, give **Home James** a call. In under 30 minutes a young man in a natty uniform (and, most likely, a fake British accent) will show up on a little Di Blasi scooter. He'll fold up the scooter, pop it in your trunk, and take you—and your car—safely home. Summon them at (213) 347-0155 or www.homejames.com.

EMERGENCIES & PERSONAL SAFETY

In all emergencies call **911** for police, fire or ambulance assistance.

HEALTH AND INSURANCE

It's best to have insurance—both health and basic travel insurance—as a hospital visit in California can be quite expensive if you don't have coverage. You may want to check with your credit card company or bank regarding basic insurance. There are also a variety of companies that offer quotes on travel insurance online to international travellers.

EMERGENCY ROOMS

Los Angeles County + USC Medical Center (LAC+USC) 1200 N. State St., (323) 226-6501. **Off map p. 9, 4-B**

Cedars-Sinai Medical Center 8700 Beverly Blvd., (310) 423-8780 or (800) CEDARS-1. **Map p. 88, 1B**

Kaiser Permanente 1526 N. Edgemont St., (323) 783-5164. **Map p. 87, 4B**

Martin Luther King/Drew Emergency Unit 12021 Wilmington Ave., (310) 668-4519. **Off map**

If you need medical care but don't have insurance or the means to pay for a hospital visit, try one of the branches of the Los Angeles Free Clinic. This non-profit provides medical, dental, HIV testing and counselling. For appointments call: (323) 653-1990. You can also walk in at any of the three branches in the city (call for locations).

In a city full of alternative therapies (want to try a light-vision radioflux treatment?) even acupuncture is available on the cheap. Yo San University, a four-year school teaching traditional Chinese medicine, holds a clinic open to the public. The first, two-hour visit is $50 and subsequent visits are $30. For seniors, all visits are $20. For appointments, call (310) 577-3006. The Santa Monica clinic is located at 13315 W. Washington Blvd. (off map p. 43, 4B).

Low-cost acupuncture is also available at Downtown's Sino-American

Medical Research Association's University of Oriental Medicine, the country's oldest school of acupuncture. The first, two-hour visit is $30, follow-up visits are $20 and 45 minutes. For appointments, call (213) 482-5000. The clinic is located at 600 St. Paul Ave (Map p. 9, 1B).

LOST AND FOUND

Lost property at LAX is handled by the Airport Police: (310) 417-0440
Lost and Found at the MTA for city buses and subways: (323) 937-8920

CONSULATES

Australian Consulate General Century Plaza Towers, 2049 Century Park East, (310) 229 4800.

British Consulate General 11766 Wilshire Blvd. #1200, (310) 481-0031

Canadian Consulate General 550 S Hope St., (213) 346-2700

Netherlands Consulate General 11766 Wilshire Blvd., (310) 268-1598

TRAVELLERS WITH DISABILITIES

Los Angeles is well-equipped for disabled travellers. More recently building codes and strict enforcement have required all new construction to be completely accessible, including parking spaces near the entrance, easy access to entrances, accessible bathrooms and telephones, cinema seats, and buses with lifts.

All LA city buses are equipped with wheelchair lifts and airports can provide wheelchairs.

Call Oscar offers door-to-door service. All vehicles are equipped with a wheelchair lift: (877) 225-5672.

USEFUL THINGS TO KNOW

INTERNET CENTRES

Los Angeles public libraries offer free internet. It's a popular service, so be prepared to wait.

Los Angeles Central Library 630 W. Fifth St., (213) 228-7000. **Map p. 9, 2B**

Beverly Hills Public Library 444 N. Rexford Dr., (310) 288-2220. **Map p. 44, 3C**

Paid access is available at many internet cafes and coffeeshops. **Cyber Java** is close to the Hollywood/Highland stop on the Metro Red Line, 7080 Hollywood Blvd., (323) 466-5600. **Map p. 86, 4B**

Rooms Cafe 1783 Westwood Blvd., (310) 445 3320. This is a quirky Japanese coffeeshop that doubles as a gallery. **Off map**

Insomnia Café 7286 Beverly Blvd., (323) 931-4943. Near some excellent shopping and dining, a favourite of aspiring screenwriters and tired UCLA students. There is a single computer for public use, but you can also bring a laptop and connect (wireless available). Bring cash, as they don't accept credit or debit cards. **Map p. 88, 4B**

California Welcome Center is the state tourist office located in the Beverly Center, 8500 Beverly Blvd. Suite 150, (310) 854-7616. **Map p. 88, 2B**

Once in a while you do get something for nothing. Here's some free internet in two appealing places:

Lounge at REDCAT in the Disney Concert Hall 631 W. 2nd. St., (213) 237-2800. Attached to the hall, this space has both an excellent gallery and a small bar/coffeeshop/bookstore that is open all day—it's a great secret hideaway from the downtown summer heat. **Map p. 9, 2B**

Newsroom Café A tasty restaurant with vegan options across the street from the celebrity-gazing restaurant Ivy. 120 N. Robertson Blvd., (310) 652-4444. **Map p. 88, 1B**

If you have your own laptop, many places in the city offer WiFi. Downtown, Pershing Square and the Central Library provide free WiFi while many coffeeshops offer paid access.

WEB RESOURCES

OFFICIAL

Los Angeles Convention and Visitor's Bureau
http://www.visitlosangeles.info

CA Tourism Office http://gocalif.ca.gov/state/tourism/tour_homepage.jsp

Los Angeles County Metropolitan Transportation Authority

http://www.mta.net

MUSEUMS, ENTERTAINMENT & GENERAL INFO

ArtScene www.artscenecal.com

La.Com www.la.com

Los Angeles Citysearch http://losangeles.citysearch.com

About Los Angeles City Guides

http://gocalifornia.about.com/cs/losangeles/a/laarticles.htm

TOURIST OFFICES

Downtown Los Angeles Visitor Information Center 685 S. Figueroa St. (between Wilshire Blvd. and 7th St.), (213) 689-8822, www.visitlosangeles.info and www.experiencela.com. Open weekdays, 9 am–5 pm. The city's official tourist centre offers maps, information on hotels, restaurants, sightseeing, discounts and event information. A second branch is located in Hollywood. **Map p. 9, 1C**

Hollywood Visitor Information Center 6801 Hollywood Blvd. [at Hollywood and Highland], (323) 467-6412, www.visitlosangeles.info. Open 10 am–10 pm, Mon–Sat; until 7 pm on Sun. **Map p. 87, 1B**

A few cities run their own visitor centres.

Beverly Hills (800) 345-2210, www.beverlyhillsbehere.com. The website offers suggested itineraries, a history of the city and a list of ongoing events.

Pasadena (626) 795-9311, www.pasadenacal.com. Pasadena's site has a good listing of self-guided architecture tours as well as Rose Bowl info.

Pentimento at LACMA

Santa Monica (800) 544-5319, www.santamonica.com. If you have friends who are residents of Santa Monica, have them book you a hotel room through the city's 'extra room' holiday special, which offers substantial discounts to locals with ID. There is an extensive visitor's guide on the site.

West Hollywood (800) 368-6020, www.visitwesthollywood. A good guide to the city's vibrant gay community, plus a comprehensive listing of the shops and galleries on the Avenues of Art and Design (Beverly, Robertson and Melrose between La Cienega and Doheny).

LOCAL PUBLICATIONS

The Los Angeles Times is the major daily newspaper.

The LA Weekly is a free alternative paper with extensive calendar listings.

Los Angeles Magazine is a monthly glossy with good calendar picks and frequent Best of LA issues.

LA Observed is a blog maintained by journalist Kevin Roderick that gives an inside take on news stories. www.laobserved.com

MUSEUM PASSES

There are no citywide museum passes, but most museums offer discounted tickets to seniors, students, and children. Many museums also have a free admission day, either once a week or once a month.

MONEY

ATMs (Automatic Teller Machines) are the easiest places to get cash and generally offer a better exchange rate than exchange offices, but make sure your card is authorised for international transactions. Debit cards are widely accepted for retail transactions.

OPENING HOURS

Museums are usually open 11 am–7 pm all week but are closed one weekday (varies by institution). Almost all museums are closed on public holidays. Galleries are open roughly 11 am–6 pm, Tue–Sat, but this can vary widely.

Malls and large shops are usually open 10 am–9 pm, Mon–Sat; 11 am–7 pm, Sun. There may be longer hours during December for Christmas shopping. Shops are hardly ever closed, except for Thanksgiving Day (the fourth Thursday in November) and Christmas Day. Smaller shops are usually open 11 am–6 pm, Mon–Sat, and are more likely to be closed on holidays.

PUBLIC HOLIDAYS

January 1	New Year's Day
January, 3rd Mon	Martin Luther King Jr Day
February, 3rd Mon	Presidents' Day
May, last Mon	Memorial Day
July 4	Independence Day
September, 1st Mon	Labor Day
October, 2nd Mon	Columbus Day
November 11	Veterans' Day
November, 4th Thur	Thanksgiving
December 25	Christmas Day

SALES TAX

California state sales tax is currently 8.25%. This is not equivalent to VAT in Europe, and there are no rebates.

TELEPHONE AND POSTAL SERVICES

Public telephones are easy to find at street corners and gas stations. Most are coin operated, but you can make operator-assisted long-distance calls.

A tri-band GSM phone will work in the US but a dual-band GSM 900/1800 MHz standard phone will not. Most US cellular carriers operate on a CDMA, TDMA or AMPS network.

The **US country code** is +1, so to reach the US from the UK dial: 00 +1 (area code) (local number)

The **international prefix** to make a call outside the US is +011, so to reach the UK from the US dial 011 +44 (area code) (local number)

Dialling 411 gives you directory service. To find a Post Office near you, call (800) ASK-USPS or view www.usps.gov.

LOCAL AREA CODES

Dial 1 + the area code + the seven-digit number

(310) Beach towns, Brentwood, Beverly Hills, Culver City, parts of West Hollywood

(323) Silverlake/Los Feliz, Hollywood, parts of West Hollywood

(213) Downtown, Echo Park, parts of Koreatown

(626) Pasadena

(818) San Fernando Valley, parts of San Gabriel Valley

TIME

Los Angeles is in the Pacific Standard Time (PST) zone, GMT-8. Daylight saving begins for most of the US at 2 am on the first Sunday of April and ends at 2 am on the last Sunday of October.

TIPPING

The following are standard tips. Of course, you should use your discretion.

Cab driver: 15%

Limousine driver: $5 or 15%, unless a service charge is already included

Valet parking attendant: $1-$5

Doorman: $1 if he hails a cab

Bellman: $5 in a five-star hotel, $1-$2 per bag elsewhere

Room service: 15%, unless a service charge is already included.

Concierge: $5 if service exceptional

Waiter: 15% of pre-tax total. Many restaurants will include a service charge for large parties, in which an extra tip is not necessary.

Sommelier: 10% based on total wine bill, less if it's an expensive vintage

Bartender: $1 per round for bottled beers, $1 per drink for serious cocktails

Coat check: $1 per item

Restroom attendant: 50¢-$1 per visit

WEIGHTS & MEASURES

The US uses the Imperial system.

STANDARD CONVERSIONS

Length	**Weight**	**Volume**
1 inch = 2.54 cm	1 ounce = 28 g	1 cup = 0.24 L
1 foot = 30 cm	1 pound = 0.45 kg	1 pint = 0.47 L
1 mile = 1.6 km	1 quart = 0.95 L	
	1 gallon = 3.8 L	

Temperature		
32°F = 0°C	68°F = 20°C	86°F = 30°C
50°F = 10°C	75°F = 24°C	95°F = 35°C

PLACES TO STAY

DOWNTOWN

$$ **Figueroa Hotel** 939 S. Figueroa St. [at Olympic Blvd.], (213) 627-8971, www.figueroahotel.com. Conveniently near the Staples Center, with Moroccan decor and individually furnished rooms. **Map p. 9, 1C**

$$$ **Standard Downtown** 550 S. Flower St. [at 6th St.], (213) 892-8080, www.standardhotel.com. A popular nightspot, with a scenic rooftop pool and sleek rooms. **Map p. 9, 1B**

Westin Bonaventure 404 S. Figueroa St. [at 4th St.], (213) 624-1000, www.westin.com. Almost worth it for the spectacular glass elevator ride, with a revolving rooftop lounge; decent but unremarkable rooms. **Map p. 9, 1B**

$$$$ Regal Biltmore 506 S. Grand Ave. [at 5th St.], 213-624-1011, www.biltmorehotel.com. Since this historic building opened in 1923 is has housed heads of state and hidden the Beatles from rabid fans. Ornate ballroom and lobby, but mediocre rooms. **Map p. 9, 2B**

The New Otani Hotel & Gardens 120 S. Los Angeles St. [at 1st St.], (213) 629-1200, www.newotani.com. In Little Tokyo near the Disney Concert Hall; some traditional Japanese tatami rooms available. **Map p. 9, 3B**

HOLLYWOOD & MIDTOWN

$$ Beverly Laurel Motor Hotel 8018 Beverly Blvd. [at Edinburgh Ave.], (323) 651-2441. Attached to Swingers, a popular 24-hour diner, this basic and affordable motel still has an element of cool. **Map p. 88, 4B**

Farmer's Daughter 115 S. Fairfax Ave. [at 1st St.], (323) 937-3930, www.farmersdaughter.com. Call it gingham-chic, or maybe farmhouse nouveau—well-kept, with a helpful staff and within walking distance of the Farmers Market and LACMA. **Map p. 88, 4B**

$$$ The Argyle 8358 W. Sunset Blvd. [near Kings Rd.], (323) 654-7100, www.argylehotel.com. Even standard rooms have classic Art Deco touches in this recently renovated 1929 gem with rooms overlooking the Sunset Strip. **Map p. 86, 2C**

Chateau Marmont 8221 W. Sunset Blvd. [at Marmont Lane], (323) 666-1010, www.chateaumarmont.com. A French chateau that looms over the Sunset Strip. The bungalows of the Chateau Marmont have been the preferred hiding place for Hollywood since 1929. **Map p. 86, 2C**

Hotel Bamboo 2528 Dearborn Drive [at Winans Drive], (323) 962-0233. Pretend you live in the Hollywood Hills with a room in this inviting, Zen-flavoured guest house. Inconvenient for walkers, but perfect if you have wheels. **Off map p. 87, 2A**

Roosevelt Hotel 7000 Hollywood Blvd. [at Orange Drive]. (323) 466-9376, www.hollywoodroosevelt.com. The very first Oscars were held here. A 2004 renovation has updated the formerly shabby rooms. The desirability of the location depends on how you feel about the tourist scrum of Hollywood Blvd. **Map p. 87, 1B**

BEVERLY HILLS & THE WESTSIDE

$$$ **The Avalon Hotel** 9400 W. Olympic Blvd. [at Canon Drive], (800) 670-6183, www.avalonbeverlyhills.com. A sleek boutique hotel with poolside dining and a sophisticated bar scene. **Map p. 44, 4D**

The Crescent 403 N. Crescent Drive [at Brighton Way], (310) 247-0505, www.crescentbh.com. Intimate 40-room hotel in the heart of Beverly Hills, with an increasingly popular outdoor bar/lounge. **Map p. 44, 3C**

Maison 140 140 Lasky Drive [at Durant Drive], (800) 670-6182, www.maison140beverlyhills.com. Hollywood Regency style gets a gorgeous update at this cosy hotel, once owned by silent screen star Lillian Gish. **Map p. 44, 2D**

The Mosaic 125 S. Spalding Drive [at Wilshire Blvd.], (310) 278-0303, www.mosaichotel.com. Brand new in Beverly Hills, offers affordable luxury in an excellent location. **Map p. 44, 2D**

$$$$ **Four Seasons** 300 S. Doheny Drive [at 3rd St.], (310) 273-2222, www.fourseasons.com. Formal and deluxe; not within easy walking distance of shops or restaurants. **Map p. 88, 1B**

W Los Angeles 930 Hilgard Ave. [near Le Conte Ave.], (310) 208-8765, www.whotels.com. Boutique chain is no longer an oxymoron; this W, tucked away on a quiet residential street, provides easy access to UCLA and Westwood. **Map p. 45, 3C**

SANTA MONICA & VENICE

$$$ **The Ambrose** 1255 20th St. [at Arizona Ave.], (310) 315-1555, www.ambrosehotel.com. Arts and Crafts meets Orientalia in this lovely Santa Monica hotel. Located on a residential street not far from the shops and eats of Montana Ave. **Map p. 42, 2B**

The Cadillac Hotel 8 Dudley Ave. [at Ocean Front Walk], (310) 399-8876, www.thecadillachotel.com. Once the summer home of Charlie Chaplin, this pink-and-turquoise Art Deco hotel is the perfect way to experience Venice Beach. **Map p. 43, 2D**

Venice Beach House Historic Inn 15 30th Ave. [at Speedway St.], (310) 823-1966, www.venicebeachhouse.com. Built as a home in 1911 by the owners of the Los Angeles Daily Journal, each room is named after a local figure (evangelist Aimee Semple MacPherson gets a whole suite!) or landmark. **Off map p. 43, 4D**

$$$$ Casa Del Mar 1910 Ocean Way [at Pico Blvd.], (310) 581-5533, www.hotelcasadelmar.com. Built in the tradition of grand seaside resorts, this elegant hotel is right on the sand, between the Venice Boardwalk and the Santa Monica Pier. **Map p. 42, 4D**

Viceroy 1819 Ocean Ave. [at Vicente Terrace], (800) 670-6185, www.viceroysantamonica.com. Over-the-top Hollywood Regency-inspired decor has made this a quick nightlife favourite. The fun extends to the colourful rooms, many with ocean views. **Map p. 42, 4D**

art glossary

Abstract Expressionism The first genuinely American movement that influenced the European art world was born after World War II. Abstract Expressionism equated the act of painting with the painting itself, where the canvas recorded a stream-of-consciousness process rather than an object as an end in itself. Jackson Pollock was the most famous artist of this school; other prominent artists, in varying degrees of figurative to abstract, include Willem de Kooning, Franz Kline and Helen Frankenthaler.

Art Deco Created in the first flush of a utopian belief in speed, industry, and the Jazz Age of the 1920s and 1930s, Art Deco took inspiration from abstract geometry rather than organic forms. There are many examples of Art Deco buildings along Wilshire Blvd. in Los Angeles, most notably Bullock's Wilshire, once a department store, now a law school library, and the Wiltern Theater, which retains many original details, down to elevator buttons with triangular motifs like arrows rushing skyward.

Art Nouveau Art Nouveau was a graphic and decorative style that grew out of the Romanticism and Symbolism of the late 19th and early 20th centuries. Art Nouveau celebrated a romantic ideal of nature, and is often characterised by intricately stylised forms of leaves, flowers and vines.

Arts and Crafts Movement Began by William Morris in England in the 1950s, the Arts and Crafts Movement was a rejection of the new industrialisation and mass production that Morris saw as destroying the environment and degrading the worker. The Arts and Crafts movement hoped to bring back local craftsmanship with forms derived from the structure of the piece and inspiration from vernacular traditions.

Bauhaus A utopian school of architecture, art and design in Dessau, Germany, founded in 1919 by the architect Walter Gropius. The Bauhaus boasted a star set of teachers, including Klee, Kandinsky, Albers and Moholy-Nagy, and promoted the International Style in architecture, where buildings were envisioned as pure objects that could be mass-produced and inserted in any locale. This rationale led to both the beautifully detailed (and surprisingly lush) buildings of Mies van der Rohe and many offensively bland office towers being built today. When the school was closed by the Nazis in 1933, many of its professors emigrated to the United States.

Beaux Art Named after the École des Beaux-Arts in Paris, this lavish style emerged in the late 19th C with variations on classical forms such as paired columns and layered motifs, and rich ornamentation illustrating garlands, wreaths, and human figures.

Blue Four (*Blaue Vier*) An alliance formed in 1924 by four painters, Paul Klee, Wassily Kandinsky, Lyonel Feininger and Alexei von Jawlensky, who met at the Bauhaus in Weimar and later held group exhibitions in Germany, Mexico and the United States. The name alludes to their former association with Blue Rider (*Blaue Reiter*), a German Expressionist group.

Case Study Houses An experimental building programme initiated by John Entenza and his *Arts and Architecture* magazine from 1945–62. Entenza foresaw the coming post-war housing shortage and hoped to showcase architects with mass customisation. Thirty-six houses were designed by such luminaries as Neutra, Eames, Ellwood and Koenig, but not all were built, due to lack of actual sites or clients. In terms of producing design that would be affordable to the general public, the programme was more successful in selling furniture than houses.

Conceptualism A broad movement that emphasises concept over form and discards the traditional view of the precious art object. The term was first used in a 1960s publication by Fluxus, a group that produced mixed media collages and guerilla theatre. Conceptualism is heavily rooted in discourse, with a high degree of reflexivity. A typical work is Joseph Kosuth's 'One and Three Chairs', which consists of a folding chair, a photograph of a chair, and a photographic enlargement of a dictionary definition of a chair.

Cubism One of the most influential art movements of the 20th C, Cubism was begun by Pablo Picasso and Georges Braque in 1907. Cubism drew on African sculpture and the paintings of Paul Cezanne, who said that artists should treat nature 'in terms of the cylinder, the sphere and the cone.' The revolutionary step of Cubism was to fracture the subject into abstract pieces which were reassembled to present a single work with multiple perspectives.

Dada The practical-joke-pulling brother to Surrealism, Dada ridiculed the museum and the very idea of enshrining artistic movements. Reacting to bourgeois values in the wake of World War I, Dadaists produced works both cynical and irrational, in some cases using accident as a means of production. Some of the most well known works are Marcel Duchamp's *Fountain* (a signed urinal) and *L.H.O.O.Q.* (a reproduction of the Mona Lisa with a faint pencil moustache).

Charles and Ray Eames Husband-and-wife design team who were a strong force in Mid-Century Modernism. The Eames built one of the most famous Case Study Houses, the Eames House in Pacific Palisades, which is characterised by its open plan, steel frame and cheerfully coloured panels. The Eames branched out into furniture (most notably their moulded plywood chairs designed for Herman Miller), short films (including *Powers of Ten*, a tour of the universe from molecule to galaxy), museum exhibitions, and objects (House of Cards, a building pack of cards).

Earth Art Begun in the late 1960s and early 1970s, coinciding with the ecological movement, Earth Art literally uses earth as material and canvas, and pulls the work—and the visitor—out of the gallery. The most famous work in Robert Smithson's *Spiral Jetty*, a huge spiral of stones projecting into the Great Salt Lake. It disappeared for a few years and only recently emerged as the water receded due to drought. Earth Art is often made with slowness in mind, dealing with issues of natural processes, erosion, and solar and lunar cycles. Other examples include Walter de Maria's *Lightning Field* and James Turrell's *Roden Crater* (still under construction).

Fauvism At the 1905 Salon d'Automne in Paris, an art critic was shocked by the irreverent and (at that time) nearly violent colors of Henri Matisse's *Green Stripe*, a portrait of Mme. Matisse. The critic dubbed it the work of 'wild beasts'; the name of Fauves stuck, although the movement was short-lived. Andre Derain, Raoul Dufy and Maurice de Vlaminck were other Fauves.

Frank Gehry Los Angeles-based architect known for swooping, off-kilter buildings, prominent from the 1980s through the present day. The 'Bilbao Effect' refers both to the museum-building boom after the unexpected success of Gehry's Guggenheim Bilbao and the way in which modern museum buildings often upstage the collections. The recently completed and very shiny Disney Concert Hall (see p. 16) in downtown LA is his most visible work in his home city, but his own house, tucked away on a Santa Monica side street, is one of the most significant (see p. 68).

Googie Named after a Googie's coffee shop with boomerang arches, designed by John Lautner in 1949. Googie-style futuristic flying angles, cantilevers and pop signage thrived in 1950s and 1960s carwashes, bowling alleys and restaurants, reflecting the booming suburban lifestyle and car love of that era. For more about Googie, see box on p. 63.

Greene & Greene Two brothers whose father decided that both should be architects, attend MIT, and then move to California. On the way there, they passed through Chicago and stopped at the World's Columbian Exhibition. There, for the first time, they saw examples of Japanese architecture. Their enthusiasm for the style would become a strong influence on their later designs. Charles and Henry built numerous Craftsman bungalows in Pasadena, with exposed beams and rafters inspired by the Japanese art of wood joinery; the most famous is the Gamble House.

David Hockney A British transplant whose residence in Los Angeles is reflected in his work, Hockney is a painter who draws, photographs, designs and theorises. Hockney's subject matter ranges from swimming pools to lounging young men to local scenery, such as the colourful *Mulholland Drive*, which is meant to evoke the experience of driving as well as the road itself. Hockney's photocollages, such as *Pearblossom Highway*, have also been widely influential.

Arata Isozaki A Japanese architect, Isozaki rose to prominence in the Post-Modernist arena of the 1970s. Isozaki's work is characterised by his use of simple geometrical forms such as cubes and grids, and bold colours; both are on display in his building for the Museum of Contemporary Art in LA, with its barrel-vault roof (an Isozaki trademark) and pyramidal skylights (see p. 11).

John Lautner Lautner arrived in LA in 1938 as an apprentice to Frank Lloyd Wright. His solo career was influenced by Wright's organic and site-specific approach, but took its own crazy turn from there. His futuristic houses, with their circular concrete walls and sweeping views, are frequently seen as the lairs of stylish movie villains. One of his most famous works is the Chemosphere, a treetop nest supported by a single column, visible from Mulholland Drive (see p. 63).

Richard Meier A New York-based architect who, by his own admission, is most well-known for using the colour white. This white often comes in grids of enamel panels and punctuated by much glass, firmly in the Modernist tradition and with a nod to Le Corbusier's curves. The much-talked-about Getty Center (see p. 48) is no exception, but with blocks of travertine, both polished and rough, floating in the sea of white.

Mission style In 1769, Father Junipero Serra helped establish a string of missions along the Camino Real, a road stretching from San Diego to San Francisco. The visually distinct style of the missions, with their Spanish tile roofs, thick stucco walls and arched entries, soon became adapted for residential construction. The Anglo appropriation of Mission style architecture reflects both an adaptation to the local climate and a romanticised view of LA's history.

Modernist Architecture and Design Modernism's clean lines are an honest expression of function, material and structure, and a rejection of the excess decorations of historical precedent. This has led to liberal use of exposed concrete, metal and glass, and the free plan, creating the sense of space through cantilevers, glass corners and slender columns in place of heavy load-bearing walls. Two dictates of this style are Chicago architect Louis Sullivan's 'Form follows function' and Mies van der Rohe's 'Less is more.'

Eric Owen Moss An LA-based architect and head of the Southern California Institute of Architecture (SciARC). Moss' buildings are primarily found within walking distance of each other in Culver City (see p. 46). All of the buildings share a capricious quality, some with their expressionist forms and carved out voids, others with structural oddities—trusses ending in mid-air and columns for the sake of columns, not support. Try to find an unlocked staircase and you'll be rewarded with a sweeping view of LA.

Neo-Classicism A style that emerged in reaction to the decadent Baroque of the mid-18th C. By using classical forms seen to be beautiful through their very mathematical and structural relationship, Neo-classicists hoped to also revive the ideals of ancient Greece and Rome. In the United States, the Neo-classical style was widely adopted for government buildings.

Richard Neutra An Austrian emigrant to LA in the 1920s, Neutra was one of the most internationally influential LA Modernists. One of his most significant works is the Lovell Health House, inspired by the regional climate and post-and-beam construction. Neutra integrated house and garden to create seamless interior/exterior spaces, tying it into its hillside site and providing sweeping views through the extensive use of glass walls.

Claes Oldenberg A New-York-based artist who got his start in the Lower East Side art scene of the 1960s making everyday objects soft—a droopy drum set, a useless vinyl payphone. In the 1970s Oldenburg and collaborator Coosje van Bruggen took the same objects and made them huge, creating a gigantic retractable lipstick on Yale's campus and an inhabitable pair of binoculars for the Frank Gehry designed Chiat/Day offices in Santa Monica (see p. 68).

Ed Ruscha The Hollywood sign is echoed in this LA-based artist's paintings and watercolours of floating text made out of various materials, from gunpowder to egg yolk. Ruscha's gaze encompasses gas stations and swimming pools, every building on the Sunset Strip (in an eponymous book of photographs), and imagines a quietly burning *Los Angeles Museum of Art on Fire*.

Rudolph Schindler Another Austrian emigrant to LA in the 1920s, Schindler's influence was more limited than Neutra's, but the

Schindler House remains one of the most subtly radical and beautiful houses in Modernist history. Built for two couples, the house is a double of itself, with two living areas, two outdoor fireplaces and gardens, and—due to Schindler's immediate embrace of Southern California climate—two sleeping porches for summer nights.

Streamline Moderne A 1930s, Art Deco architectural style, Streamline Moderne drew upon forms of modern transportation such as airplanes and automobiles to create a sense of movement and speed. It is characterised by horizontal lines, with narrow bands of windows in imitation of ocean liners, and round corners creating an aerodynamic feel. A notable example is the old May Co. department store on Wilshire, now annexed by the Los Angeles County Museum of Art (see p. 90). The new shell of the Hollywood Bowl (see p. 99) is based on a Streamline Moderne design by Lloyd Wright, the son of Frank Lloyd Wright.

Frank Lloyd Wright Possibly the most influential American architect, Wright created the Usonian and Prairie styles, which were characterised by low proportions and large overhangs tying the house to the ground, emphasising the relationship between the building and nature and the need for site-specific design. One of his most famous buildings was Fallingwater, with a house cantilevered over a waterfall. In later years, Wright was inspired by pre-Columbian architecture and began a series of concrete textile block houses, which can be seen at Barnsdall Park and La Miniatura. For more about Frank Lloyd Wright in Los Angeles, see p. 78.

index

Page numbers in italics indicate Art Glossary references.

art/shop/eat Los Angeles

First edition, 2005

Published by Blue Guides Limited, a Somerset Books company
The Studio, 51 Causton Street, London SW1P 4AT

ISBN 1-905131-06-2

Published in the United States of America by
WW Norton & Company, Inc
500 Fifth Avenue, New York, NY 10110, USA

ISBN 0-393-32782-5

Editor: Maya Mirsky
Copy editing: Mark Griffith
Layout: Attila György, Ila Wolf
Volume design: Anikó Kuzmich and Regina Rácz
Series devised by Gemma Davies

Printed and bound by M.G.I. Print in China.

The author would like to thank Margaret Wappler (Silverlake, Los Feliz and Echo Park), Krystal Chang, Henry Jackman and intern Krishanti Wahla for their invaluable assistance.